GREEK HISTORICAL DOCUMENTS

GREEK HISTORICAL DOCUMENTS

THE FIFTH CENTURY B.C.

NAPHTALI LEWIS

A.M. HAKKERT, LTD., TORONTO

1971

Set in Aldine Roman
by Ancient and Modern Book Printers
Toronto, Canada
Printed in The Netherlands

Standard Book Numbers
Cloth: 88866-503-2
Paper: 88866-504-0

Library of Congress Catalogue Card Number
75-148096

A. M. Hakkert Ltd.
76 Charles Street West
Toronto 5, Ontario

TO
JUDY AND JOHN

λαμπάδια ἔχοντες διαδώσουσιν

CONTENTS

PREFACE

Athens is the succinct but eloquent title of the Cambridge Ancient History's fifth volume, which covers the fifth century B.C. The same emphasis will be apparent in the present collection of documents. The extant fifth-century documents, like the extant fifth-century literature, relate preponderantly to Athens.

Whether preserved as inscriptions on stone (occasionally bronze) or as quotations in contemporary or later writers, ancient documents, like ancient literature, are subject to the hazards of survival. Our knowledge of antiquity is correspondingly fragmentary and lacunose. Since stone was used for permanent records (other materials, such as papyrus and wooden tablets, served more temporary purposes), the inscribed documents are — aside from funerary monuments — mostly of an official or public nature. Consequently, the inscriptions of fifth-century date are a unique source of information on such subjects as foreign relations and domestic policies, the technical details and procedures of government, treaty-making and legislation, the tribute of the Delian Confederacy and Athens' treatment of the member states, the building of the Parthenon and the Erechtheion, the financing of the Peloponnesian War. The present volume includes examples of inscriptions which contribute significantly to our knowledge of these subjects.

As for literary sources, the authors and works that constitute our prime sources of fifth-century history — Herodotos, Thucydides, Plato, Aristophanes, Plutarch's *Lives* — are readily available in libraries and in paperback reprints. Accordingly, except for a number of treaties reported by Thucydides, these principal authors are omitted from the present volume, and space has been given instead to lesser lights like Diodoros of Sicily and Pseudo-Xenophon, who furnish important information that the reader is less likely to encounter otherwise.

The following excerpts are reprinted by permission of the publishers and the Loeb Classical Library: C. H. Oldfather's translation of Diodoros of Sicily Vol. IV, Book 11, chaps. 11, 54-55, 63-64, 67-68 and 87, George Norlin's translation of Isocrates Vol. I, *Panegyricus* 103-6 and 115-20, Harold North Fowler's translation of Plutarch's *Moralia* Vol. X, 835C-836A, and C. Forster Smith's translation of Thucydides Vols. II, III, IV, Book 4, chaps. 118-19, Book 5, chaps. 18-19 and 23-24, Book 8, chaps. 18, 37 and 58 — all Cambridge, Mass., Harvard University Press. R. F. Willetts' translation of the Laws of Gortyn is reproduced with the permission of the publisher, Walter De Gruyter & Co., Berlin. The quotations from R. Meiggs and D. Lewis, *A Selection of Greek Historical Inscriptions to the End of the Fifth Century,* are included with the permission of the publisher, the Clarendon Press, Oxford. The treatises on the constitutions of Athens and Sparta are given in the translation of H. G. Dakyns (London, 1890), revised by me. All other translations are my own.

May 1970   NAPHTALI LEWIS

A NOTE ON SPELLING AND ABBREVIATIONS

From the Renaissance almost to the middle of the twentieth century it was customary to Latinize or Anglicize Greek names and terms, writing Aristotle for what in Greek was Aristoteles, Pericles for Perikles, and so forth. In recent years that practice has been increasingly abandoned by scholars in favor of simple transliteration: thus we now write Hieron instead of Hiero, Halai instead of Halae, Kleisophos instead of Clisophus, Menandros instead of Menander. This newer practice is observed in the present volume, except in individual instances where the familiarity of the older spelling is too firmly established for revision, e.g. Apollo, Thucydides and Delphi, where transliteration would yield Apollon, Thoukydides and Delphoi.

Inscriptions are cited by their numbers in the following collections of epigraphical texts; in cases where the inscription is available in more than one source, the source most informative to the English-speaking reader is cited.

ATL = B.D. Meritt, H.T. Wade-Gery and M.F. McGregor, *The Athenian Tribute Lists*. 4 vols., Cambridge, Mass., 1939-53.

IG = *Inscriptiones Graecae*, editio minor vol. I. Berlin, 1924.

Meiggs-Lewis = R. Meiggs and D. Lewis, *A Selection of Greek Historical Inscriptions to the End of the Fifth Century B.C.* Oxford, 1969.

Syll. = W. Dittenberger, *Sylloge Inscriptionum Graecarum*. 3d ed., 4 vols. Leipzig, 1915-24.

Tod = M.N. Tod, *A Selection of Greek Historical Inscriptions*. 2 vols. Oxford, 1946-48.

I ATHENS

ATHENIAN DECREE CONCERNING SALAMIS
Meiggs-Lewis 14

This is the earliest extant Athenian decree. Its fragmentary state leaves many details unclear, particularly the question of whether it relates to native Salaminians or to Athenian residents or cleruchs. If to cleruchs, its date is ca. 510 B.C., otherwise it may be ten or twenty years later.

The assembly decrees to allow the ... in Salamis to live in Salamis permanently, except that they must pay taxes and perform military service in Athens. They shall not lease out their landholdings in Salamis except to residents(?);[1] if anyone does, lessee and lessor shall each pay a penalty of ... to the public treasury; the (Athenian) governor shall collect it, and if not he shall be fined. They shall provide themselves with arms worth thirty drachmas, and the governor shall ... ... in the council.[2]

ATHENIAN DEDICATIONS AT DELPHI
Meiggs-Lewis 19 and 25

The first of the following texts is a later re-inscription of the original inscription that accompanied thank-offerings dedicated at Delphi after the Battle of Marathon (490 B.C.). The second is the dedicatory inscription of the portico that the Athenians erected there, perhaps as a thank-offering for the victory at Salamis (480 B.C.).

(1) The Athenians (dedicated) to Apollo the first fruits of the battle at Marathon, (taken) from the Persians.
(2) The Athenians dedicated the stoa and the armor and the akroteria (from the booty) seized from the enemy.

THEMISTOKLES' MEASURES TO MEET XERXES' INVASION
Meiggs-Lewis 23

Discovered in 1958 by Professor Michael Jameson of the University of Pennsylvania, this inscription has stirred a lively running debate over its authenticity. The opposing arguments and alignment of scholars are conveniently summarized by M. Chambers in *Philologus* 111, 1967, pp. 157-69, and in Meiggs-Lewis, pp. 50-52. The lettering of the inscription is in the style of the third century B.C., and opinion appears to be converging on the view that we have before us a later edition of the original decree of June/July 480 B.C., conflated perhaps with one or two additional texts. For later re-inscription of important earlier documents cf. pp. 3, 67, 107.

Gods. The council and assembly decree, on motion of Themistokles son of Neokles, of (the deme) Phrearrhoi:

to deposit the city in the care of Athena protectress of Athens and all the other gods to guard and ward off the barbarian in behalf of the land; and that all the Athenians and the foreigners resident in Athens deposit their children and wives in Troizen under the protection of Pittheus(?) the tutelary hero of the land, and deposit their aged and possessions in Salamis; and that the treasurers and priestesses remain on the acropolis to guard the property of the gods;

and that all the other adult Athenians and foreigners embark on the two hundred prepared ships and, together with the Spartans, Corinthians, Aiginetans and the others willing to share the danger, ward off the barbarian for the sake of their own freedom and that of the rest of the Greeks;

and that the generals, beginning tomorrow morning, appoint two hundred trierarchs — one for each ship — from amongst those possessing land and a house in Athens and having legitimate children and not older than fifty years, and assign the ships to them by lot; and (that they) choose ten marines for each ship from amongst those aged over twenty up to thirty years, and four archers; and (that they) choose by lot also the complement for the ships when they also choose by lot the trierarchs; and that the generals draw up on white boards lists also of the other(?) men by ships, the Athenians from the deme registers, the foreigners from those listed with the polemarch, and in the listing assign them at the rate of a hundred to each of the two hundred divisions, and write above each division the name of the trireme and trierarch and the complement, so that each division may know on which trireme to embark; and that when all the divisions have been (thus) distributively constituted and allotted to the triremes the council and the generals shall man fully all two hundred ships after offering a propitiatory sacrifice to Zeus all-powerful and Athena and Nike and Poseidon safe-guarder;

and when the ships have been manned, with one hundred of them to lend aid at Artemision in Euboia, and with the other hundred of them to lie in wait around Salamis and the rest of Attika and guard the land;

and, in order that all Athenians be concordant in warding off the barbarian, that those exiled for ten years go off to Salamis and remain there until the assembly decrees about them, and . . . [The rest is lost.]

THE HEROES OF THERMOPYLAI
Diodoros of Sicily 11.11

The merits of these men, who would not regard them with wonder? They with one accord did not desert the post to which Greece had assigned them, but gladly offered up their own lives for the common salvation of all Greeks, and preferred to die bravely rather than to live shamefully. The consternation of the Persians also, no one could doubt that they felt it. For what man among the barbarians could have conceived of that which had taken place? Who could have expected that a band of only five hundred ever had the daring to charge against the hundred myriads? Consequently what man of later times might not emulate the valor of those warriors who, finding themselves in the grip of an overwhelming situation, though their bodies were subdued, were not conquered in spirit? These men, therefore, alone of all of whom history records, have in defeat been accorded a greater fame than all others who have won the fairest victories. For judgement must be passed upon brave men, not by the outcome of their actions, but by their purpose; in the one case Fortune is mistress, in the other it is the purpose which wins approval. What man would judge any to be braver than were those Spartans who, though not equal in number to even the thousandth part of the enemy, dared to match their valor against the unbelievable multitudes? Nor had they any hope of overcoming so many myriads, but they believed that in bravery they would surpass all men of former times, and they decided that, although the battle they had to fight was against the barbarians, yet the real contest and the award of valor they were seeking was in competition with all who had ever won admiration for their courage. Indeed they alone of those of whom we have knowledge from time immemorial chose rather to preserve the laws of their state than their own lives, not feeling aggrieved that the greatest perils threatened them, but concluding that the greatest boon for which those who practise valor should pray is the opportunity to play a part in contests of this kind. And one would be justified in believing that it was these men who were more responsible for the common freedom of the Greeks than those who were victorious at a later time in the battles against Xerxes; for when the deeds of these men were called to mind, the Persians were dismayed whereas the Greeks were incited to perform similar courageous exploits.

And, speaking in general terms, these men alone of the Greeks down to their time passed into immortality because of their exceptional valor. Consequently not only the writers of history but also many of our poets have celebrated their brave exploits; and one of them is Simonides, the lyric poet, who composed the following encomium in their praise, worthy of their valor:

Of those who perished at Thermopylai
All glorious is the fortune, fair the doom;
Their grave's an altar, ceaseless memory's theirs
Instead of lamentation, and their fate
Is chant of praise. Such winding-sheet as this
Nor mould nor all-consuming time shall waste.
This sepulchre of valiant men has taken
The fair renown of Hellas for its inmate.
And witness is Leonidas, once king
Of Sparta, who hath left behind a crown
Of valor mighty and undying fame.[3]

THE GREEK STATES ALLIED AGAINST PERSIA
Meiggs-Lewis 27

Before dividing the spoils from their defeat of Xerxes the Greeks, according to Herodotos (9.81), reserved tithes for Apollo at Delphi, Zeus at Olympia, and Poseidon at the Isthmus. Herodotos reports further that from the tithes sent to Delphi "was dedicated the gold tripod that stands on the bronze three-headed serpent very near the altar." This bronze pedestal — formed, actually of three entwined serpents — was transported by order of Constantine the Great to Constantinople, where it still stands in the ancient Hippodrome. It is engraved with the names of the Greek states that fought in the war. A number of names, e.g. Kroton, are inexplicably missing from the list.

These fought the war: Sparta,[4] Athens, Corinth, Tegea, Sikyon, Aigina, Megara, Epidauros, Orchomenos, Phleious, Troizen, Hermione, Tiryns, Plataia, Thespiai, Mykenai, Keos, Malis, Tenos, Naxos, Eretria, Chalkis, Styra, Halieis, Potidaia, Leukas, Anaktorion, Kythnos, Siphnos, Ambrakia, Lepreon.

ATHENIAN DECREE CONCERNING ERYTHRAI
Meiggs-Lewis 40

Erythrai, an Ionian city on the coast opposite Chios, was one of the original members of the Confederacy. This decree, probably belonging to the period 470-450 B.C., illustrates how Athens infringed on the sovereignty of the allied cities, imposing democratic constitutions, increasingly requiring that major cases be tried in Athens, and substituting Athena for Apollo as the principal tutelary for all member cities. See further Meiggs-Lewis, pp. 91-93.

[The prescript is lost.]
The Erythraians shall bring to the Great Panathenaic Festival food worth not less than 3 minas, and to the Erythraians attending the overseer of rites shall distribute the meat, a drachma's worth to each. If they bring less than 3 minas' worth, food for the rites shall be purchased according to their obligations, the amount of the deficiency shall be entered in a record of debt against the government, and any one of the Erythraians so desiring may see to it.

Erythrai shall have a council of 120 men chosen by lot. The council shall examine (the qualifications of) each man so chosen: an alien may not be a councilor, nor anyone under 30 years of age, and violators (of this provision) shall be liable to prosecution. No one shall be a councilor twice within four years. The present council shall be drawn by lot and constituted by the (Athenian) overseers and garrison commander, in future by the council itself and the commander not less than thirty days before the council goes out of office. They shall swear by Zeus, Apollo and Demeter, imprecating utter destruction upon those who swear false and utter destruction upon their children. They shall swear the oath over burning sacrifices; the council shall burn sacrifices of not less than oxen, or else shall be liable to a fine of 1,000 drachmas; and when the assembly swears the assembly shall burn no less.

The council oath is as follows: "To the best and truest of my ability I will serve as councilor for the people of Erythrai and Athens and the allies. I will not revolt against the people of Athens or against the allies of Athens, either of my own accord or at the behest of another, and I will not defect, either of my own accord or at the behest of any other person at all. Of the exiles – i.e. of those who fled to the Medes – I will never receive back a single one, either of my own accord or at the behest of another, without (the authorization of) the council and assembly of Athens, nor of those who remain will I drive any out without (the authorization of) the council and assembly of Athens."

If any Erythraian kills another Erythraian, he shall be put to death if convicted; if he is condemned to exile, he shall be banished from the entire Athenian alliance, and his property shall be confiscated by Erythrai. If anyone is convicted of acting to betray the city of Erythrai to tyrants, he himself may be put to death with impunity, and also the children born of him; but if the children born of him are shown to be supporters of the government of Erythrai and that of Athens, they shall be spared, and after forfeiting all his property they shall receive back half and half shall be confiscated.

[The rest of the inscription is fragmentary.]

THE TRIBUTE ASSESSMENTS
OF THE ATHENIAN CONFEDERACY
ATL 1 and 14 (= *IG* 191 and 204)

In 454 B.C., on the ground that Delos was too exposed to the revitalized Persian fleet, the Athenians transferred the treasury of the Delian League to the safekeeping of their own acropolis (where it was subsequently put to such purely Athenian uses as helping to pay for building the Parthenon). Out of each city's annual tribute one sixtieth was donated to Athena. Lists of these "first fruits for the goddess" were inscribed annually and publicly displayed at Athens. Fragments of these inscriptions — from which, of course, a city's actual tribute can readily be calculated — are extant for each year from 454/3 to 432/1 B.C. and for a dozen later years down to 406/5, the last year in which the tribute was collected. The annual assessment for each member state varied with its size, importance and presumed ability to pay. Initially the usual range extended from a low of 100 drachmas to a high of 12 talents, with a group of Hellespontine cities paying 18 talents and Byzantion alone paying 18 talents 1800 drachmas (Chios, Lemnos and Samos contributed ships as well). In 425 B.C., to help defray the cost of the Peloponnesian War, the tribute was increased from an annual total of 400 talents or less to a figure in the neighborhood of 1500 talents. A translation of a reconstructed text of the decree imposing the increased assessments is given in B. D. Meritt and A. B. West, *The Athenian Assessment of 425 B.C.* (Ann Arbor, 1934), pp. 47-50 (that reconstruction has since been modified in a number of details: see Meiggs-Lewis, below).

Excellent summaries of what we learn from the extant fragments of these lists are to be found in Meiggs-Lewis, pp. 83-88 and 193-99. An exhaustive study of these and related inscriptions is available in B. D. Meritt, H. T. Wade-Gery and M. F. McGregor, *The Athenian Tribute Lists* (4 vols., Cambridge, Mass., 1939-53). A synoptic tabulation of the tribute for the years before the Peloponnesian War is presented in G. F. Hill, *Sources for Greek History between the Persian and Peloponnesian Wars*. New edition by R. Meiggs and A. Andrewes (Oxford, 1951).

Given below are the preamble used in the first year, 454/3 B.C. (in subsequent years a brief dating caption sufficed), followed by a summary and sample of one of the best preserved lists, that of 441/0. Items in the list now lost and not restorable from other evidence are indicated by —.

The following first fruits for the goddess were received from the Hellenotamiai for whom ————————— was secretary and were paid to the thirty auditors from the tribute which the cities delivered in the archonship of Aristion at Athens, (at the rate of) a mina per talent.

[Following the last few entries of what obviously was captioned "Ionian Tribute", we read:]

Hellespontine Tribute

(dr.)	(ob.)		(dr.)	(ob.)	
5		Harpagion	5		Neapolis, (colony)
200		Arisbe			from Athens
100		Dardanos	288		Tenedos
16	4	Sigeion	16	4	---
8	2	Palaiperkote	1000		Perinthos
16	4	Fort Daunion	33	2	Neandreia
16	4	Fort Didymon	16	4	Paisos
1200		Lampsakos	400		Abydos
900		Kalchedon	8	2	Priapos
16	4	Lamponeia	100		Kampsa
900		Kyzikos	33	2	Artake
300		Prokonnesos	8	2	Sestos
100		Agora-on-Chersonese	8	2	Madytos
16	4	Astakos	8	2	Limnai
1507	4	Byzantion	50		Elaious
500		Selymbria	33	2	Parion
			---		Zeleia

Thraceside Tribute

(dr.)	(ob.)		(dr.)	(ob.)	
300	---		600		Skione
600		Poteidaia	16	4	Skiathos
---	---		300		Peparethos
---	---		150		Maroneia
66	4	Mekyberna	500+(?)		Mende
50		Neapolis, (colony)	33	2	Aige
		from Mende	100		Aphytis
100		Dion-on-Athos	25		Haisa
---		Samothrace	1000		Ainos

traces	200		Olynthos
of	25		Ikos
nine	600		Torone
more	16	4	Stageira
names	16	4	Phegetos
	16	4	Othoros
	100		Argilos
	16	4	Pharbelos
	66	4	Stolos

[Next come the captions "Karian Tribute" followed by 44 entries, and "Island Tribute" followed by 24 entries.]

ECONOMIC IMPERIALISM
Meiggs-Lewis 45

In Aristophanes' *Birds,* produced in 414 B.C., the Seller of Decrees proclaims that "the people of Cloudcuckooland shall use the same measures, weights and coinage as the Olophyxians" (verses 1040-41). Behind this spoof we recognize a reference to an actual law imposed by Athens on the cities of the Confederacy ca. 450 B.C. Fragments of the law have been found at Aphytis, Cos, Smyrna, Siphnos and Syme, reflecting the provision of the decree that a copy was to be set up in every city of the Athenian empire. Different scholars have proposed various restorations of the missing portions of the text; the following translation is based for the most part on the text of Meiggs and Lewis.

[The beginning is too fragmentary for restoration.]

If any citizen or foreigner in the cities, other than the (Athenian) governors, acts contrary to this decree, he shall be disfranchised and his property shall be confiscated, a tithe going to the goddess. If there are no Athenian governors, the magistrates of the respective cities shall carry out the provisions of the decree;

and if they act contrary to the decree, a prosecution for disfranchisement shall be instituted at Athens against such magistrates.

Receiving the (foreign) money in the mint (at Athens), the managers shall convert not less than half into (Athenian) coin . . . exacting in each case a fee of three(?) drachmas per mina; the other half . . .

[Here another portion is too broken for continuous sense.]

If anyone moves or votes to decree that it be lawful to use or make a loan in foreign coinage, he shall immediately be denounced to the Eleven, and the Eleven shall punish him with death; if he disputes the charge, they shall bring him to trial.

The assembly shall choose heralds and send them to the cities to announce the (present) decree, one herald to the Islands, one to Ionia, one to the Hellespont, and one to the settlements in Thrace; the generals shall dispatch them . . . , and if not each (general) shall be fined ten thousand drachmas. The governors in the cities shall have this decree inscribed on a stone stele and erect it in the agora of each city, and (at Athens) the managers (shall erect it) in front of the mint; Athens shall carry this out if the said persons are recalcitrant, but the herald who goes shall ask them to do what Athens bids.

The secretary of the council shall in future add the following to the oath of the council: "If anyone coins silver money in the cities and does not use Athenian coins or measures or weights but foreign coins and measures and weights, I will vote the penalty and punishment in accordance with the previous decree moved by Klearchos."

Anyone is permitted to turn in the foreign money that he has and exchange it on these same terms whenever he wishes, and the city will give him Athenian coinage in exchange; each shall bring his own to Athens and deposit it at the mint. The (mint) managers shall . . . recording . . . in front of the mint for anyone so desiring to inspect . . .

[The rest is lost.]

Demosthenes, *Oration* 35 § 51

With the aim of assuring Athens' food supply from overseas a law was passed requiring Athenians and metics, under sanctions amounting to con-

fiscation, to bring all grain shipments in which they had a commercial interest
to the port of Athens. This is apparently the law from which several clauses
(but obviously not the first) are quoted by Demosthenes. Although the
genuineness of the documents inserted in the speeches of Demosthenes is
generally suspect, this one appears to have the ring of truth.

It shall be unlawful for any one of the Athenians or of the
metics residing in Athens or of those over whom they have control
to lend money on any ship whose cargo of grain[5] is not destined
for Athens. If any one makes a loan contrary to these provisions,
the deposition and the charge concerning the money shall take
place before the superintendents, following the same procedures as
stipulated above for the ship and the grain; and he shall have no
cause of action concerning the money which he lends for a
destination other than Athens, and no magistracy whatever shall
bring in an action concerning this.

COLLECTING THE TRIBUTE OF THE ATHENIAN EMPIRE
Meiggs-Lewis 46

These regulations, aimed at assuring the receipt of all the tribute due
from the cities of the Confederacy, were decreed by Athens ca. 447 B.C.
"The fluctuations in the number of cities in the annual quota lists, and the
recurrence of incomplete and double payments in the early forties show that
Athens could not rely on receiving every year all the tribute that was due to
her. This decree is an attempt to improve discipline, and the measures
approved by the Assembly are to be the responsibility of the Boule, with the
co-operation of Athenian officials overseas — travelling commissioners and
resident officials, both of whom are found in other decrees of the fifties and
forties" — Meiggs-Lewis, p. 119.

Gods. The council and the assembly decree — (the tribe)
Oineis was in prytany, Spoudias was secretary, _____on was
president, Kleinias moved —
The council and the (Athenian) governors, as well as the
visiting overseers, shall see to it that the tribute is collected each
year and is brought to Athens. They shall issue seals to the cities,
so that it will not be possible for those bringing the tribute to

perpetrate fraud; the city shall write on a tablet the tribute that it is sending, mark it with the seal, and send it to Athens; those bringing it shall deliver the tablet in the council for verification when they deliver the tribute. The prytaneis shall hold an assembly after the Dionysia[6] for the Hellenotamiai to disclose to the Athenians the cities that have delivered the tribute in full and, separately, those falling short, if any. The Athenians shall choose four men to send to the cities to give receipts for the tribute delivered, and to exact the undelivered tribute from those falling short: two men shall sail on swift triremes to the cities in the Islands and Ionia, and two to the cities in Hellespont and Thrace. The prytaneis shall bring this matter before the council and the assembly immediately after the Dionysia, and they shall deliberate on this matter uninterruptedly until it is accomplished.

[The decree continues with provisions for filing and hearing complaints of irregularities or malfeasance. The final portion of the inscription is too fragmentary for restoration.]

REBUILDING THE TEMPLE OF ATHENA NIKE
Syll. 62

This is one of two extant inscriptions containing decrees about the repair of the beautiful little temple of the "Wingless Victory" that still stands near the entrance to the acropolis. Kallikrates, mentioned here, was the architect of the Long Walls and together with Iktinos built the Parthenon. The date of this inscription is ca. 447 B.C.

. . . to build up the acropolis wall (?) so that no runaway slave or thief may enter. Kallikrates shall draw the plans so as to accomplish the work in the best and least expensive way, and the commissioner shall let the contracts so that the repair is accomplished within sixty days. The guards shall be three bowmen from the tribe in prytany.[7]

ATHENIAN DOMINATION IN EUBOIA
Meiggs-Lewis 52

In 446/5 B.C., after suppressing the secession of Euboia, Athens decreed new charters for the cities of the island. "Euboea had been crushed; but its cities, except Histiaia, were to remain separate, 'autonomous' states, members of the League, though more clearly than before controlled by Athens. The nature of that control is shown by the terms of the treaty with Chalkis, especially the last clause" — A. W. Gomme, *A Historical Commentary on Thucydides,* vol. I (Oxford, 1945), p. 342.

The council and assembly decree — (the tribe) Antiochis was in prytany, Drakontides presided, Diognetos moved —
The council (of 500) and the jurors of the Athenians shall take an oath as follows: "I will not expel the Chalkidians from Chalkis or destroy their city;[8] I will not (vote to) destroy, disfranchise, punish with exile, arrest, put to death or confiscate the property of any private citizen without trial, unless (authorized) by the government of Athens; nor will I without a formal summons take a vote either against the community of Chalkis or against any private citizen. If an embassy comes when I am prytanis, I will present it before the council and assembly within ten days insofar as possible.[9] I will uphold these provisions for the Chalkidians so long as they are obedient to the government of Athens."

An embassy coming from Chalkis shall, together with the (Athenian) commissioners of oaths, administer the oath to the Athenians and shall record (the names of) those who take the oath. The generals shall see to it that all take the oath.

The Chalkidians shall take an oath as follows: "I will not revolt against the government of Athens by any manner or means either in word or in deed, nor will I follow anyone revolting; and if anyone incites to revolt, I will denounce him to the Athenians. I will pay to the Athenians whatever tribute I may convince the Athenians (to assess). I will be the best and truest ally possible; I will aid and defend the government of Athens if anyone wrongs the government of Athens, and I will be obedient to the government of Athens."

All Chalkidians who are of age shall take the oath; any man who does not take the oath shall be disfranchised, his property

shall be confiscated, and a tithe of his property shall be consecrated (in Chalkis) to Olympian Zeus. An embassy of Athenians
coming to Chalkis shall, together with the commissioners of oaths
in Chalkis, administer the oath and shall record (the names of) the
Chalkidians who take the oath.

Antikles moved —

With the good fortune of the Athenians: The Athenians and
the Chalkidians shall ratify the oath just as the government of
Athens ordered in the case of the Eretrians.[10] The generals shall
see to it that this is done as soon as possible. The assembly shall
choose immediately five men who shall go to Chalkis and administer the oath. Concerning the hostages the answer to the Chalkidians shall be that for now the Athenians have decided to leave
matters as already decreed, but whenever it shall seem appropriate
they will reconsider and will make such changes as may seem
advantageous for Athens and Chalkis. All aliens residing in Chalkis
who do not pay taxes to Athens and have not been granted tax
exemption by the government of Athens, shall pay taxes to
Chalkis just like the other Chalkidians.

The secretary of the council shall, at the expense of the
Chalkidians, inscribe this decree and the oath at Athens on a stone
stele and shall erect it on the acropolis, and in Chalkis the council
of the Chalkidians shall inscribe and erect (a copy) in the temple
of Olympian Zeus.

Such shall be the decree for the Chalkidians. And three men
whom the council shall choose from amongst themselves shall as
soon as possible, together with Hierokles,[11] offer the sacrifices in
accordance with the oracles regarding Euboia. The generals shall
assist in seeing to it that the sacrifices are offered as soon as
possible, and shall provide the money therefor.

Archestratos moved —

In addition to Antikles' motion, the Chalkidians shall have
the right to pass sentence against their own (people) at Chalkis just
as the Athenians (have) at Athens, except for exile, death and
disfranchisement; concerning these there shall be an appeal to
Athens to the court of the Thesmothetai according to government
decree. Concerning the garrison of Euboia the generals shall see to
the best of their ability that it serves the best interests of Athens.

THE ATHENIANS COLONIZE BREA IN THRACE
Meiggs-Lewis 49

This decree, dating from ca. 445 B.C., illustrates the administrative detail that went into the founding of a Greek colony. "We know of more than a dozen settlements, colonies, and cleruchies sent out by Athens in the fifth century, and of most of them we know when they were sent, where they were sent, and, in outline, how they fared. It is a strange irony that the only settlement for which we have good contemporary evidence is the colony of Brea, whose date and site are uncertain and which for us has no history" — Meiggs-Lewis, p. 130.

[The beginning is lost.]

The colony leaders shall provide the wherewithal for offering auspicious sacrifices on behalf of the colony, as much as they deem appropriate. Ten men shall be chosen as assigners of land, one per tribe, and these shall assign the land. Demokleides shall have full power to establish the colony according to the best of his ability.

The sacred precincts already proclaimed shall remain as they are, and no others shall be consecrated. They shall contribute an ox and a panoply for the Great Panathenaia and a phallus for the Dionysia.

If anyone marches against the land of the colonists, the cities (of the region) shall come to their aid as speedily as possible in accordance with the covenants concerning the cities in Thrace executed when . . . was secretary (of the council).

These provisions shall be inscribed on a stele and placed on the acropolis, and the colonists shall provide the stele at their own expense. If anyone takes a vote contrary to (the decree on) the stele or any orator urges or supports a proposal to rescind or annul any of its provisions, he and the children born of him shall be disfranchised and his property shall be confiscated, a tithe going to the goddess; but the colonists themselves may petition (for changes).

Those of the soldiers who, when they return to Athens, enroll to be colonists, shall be at Brea to settle there within thirty days. The colony shall be led forth within thirty days, and Aischines[12] shall accompany and pay the money.

Phantokles moved —

In addition to Demokleides' motion concerning the colony at Brea, the (next?) prytany of (the tribe) Erechtheis shall present Phantokles before the council at the first session; and the colonists going to Brea shall be from the (classes of) thetes and zeugitai.

MATERIALS FOR THE ATHENA STATUE
Meiggs-Lewis 54

The chryselephantine cult statue that the sculptor Pheidias fashioned for the Parthenon was famous throughout antiquity. Spread over several years, the total cost of the statue was more than 700 talents. This inscription records the expenditure of 100 talents in 440/39 B.C. for the purchase of gold and ivory.

Gods. Athena. Fortune.

100 tal.	Kichesippos of Myrrinous was secretary of the commissioners in charge of the statue. Received from the treasurers, for whom Demostratos of Xypete was secretary, the treasurers Ktesion, Stronias, Antiphates, Menandros, Thymochares, Smokordos, Pheideleides.[13] (Expended)
Cost	Gold was purchased, weighing 6 talents,
87 tal. 4652 dr. 5 ob.	1618 drachmas, 1 obol.
2 tal. 743 dr.	Ivory was purchased . . .
	[The rest is lost.]

PARTHENON CONSTRUCTION RECORDS
Meiggs-Lewis 59

Construction of the Parthenon began in 447/6 B.C. and ended in 433/2. The work was supervised by annually elected commissioners. The accounts of each year were inscribed and displayed on the acropolis. The best preserved is the following account for the year 434/3, when the work was approaching completion.

(Accounts of) the commissioners, of whom Antikles was secretary; in the fourteenth council,[14] for which Metagenes was the first to serve as secretary; in the archonship of Krates at Athens.

Itemized receipts of this year:

1470 dr.	Surplus from the previous year
74 st.	Electrum staters of Lampsakos[15]
27 1/6 st.	Electrum staters of Kyzikos
	From the treasurers who manage the
25,000 dr.	finances of the goddess, of whom
	Krates of Lamptrai was secretary.
1372 dr.	Price of gold sold, weighing 98 dr.
1309 dr.[16]	Price of ivory sold, weighing 3 tal. 60 dr.

	Expenditures:
?[17] dr. 1 ob.	Purchases
	Contract wages
1926 dr. 2 ob.	Laborers (quarrying) at Pentele
	and loading stone on wagons
16,392 dr.	Statue makers,[18] annual wage
?[19] dr. 2 ob.	Hired by the month

	Left over from this year:
74 st.	Electrum staters of Lampsakos
27 1/6 st.	Electrum staters of Kyzikos.

TREATY BETWEEN ATHENS AND RHEGION
Meiggs-Lewis 63

As part of Perikles' policy of consolidating a sphere of influence in the Western Greek world, Athens in 433/2 B.C. concluded alliances with two Ionian settlements, Leontinoi in Sicily and Rhegion in Southern Italy. The text of the latter treaty follows; the former, also extant in part, may be found in Meiggs-Lewis 64.

Gods. The envoys from Rhegion who executed the alliance and the oath: Kleandros son of Xen_____, _____ son of _____tinos, Silenos son of Phokas, and . . . In the archonship of Apseudes and the council (year) for which Kritiades was the first to serve as secretary.

The council and assembly decree — (the tribe) Akamantis was in prytany, Charias was secretary, Timoxenos presided, Kallias moved —

An alliance shall exist between Athens and Rhegion, and the Athenians shall swear an oath so that all dealings of Athens with Rhegion may forever be in good faith, without fraud, and open, swearing as follows: "We will be faithful, just, strong and treaty-abiding allies to Rhegion forever, and we will lend aid if any need arises . . ."[20]

[The rest is lost.]

WAR LOANS
Meiggs-Lewis 72

Greek temples customarily used their funds to make interest-bearing loans. Athens financed the Peloponnesian War in part by borrowing from the temple treasuries. A long inscription records the borrowings for "the four years from Panathenaia to Panathenaia," as well as interest due in that quadrennium on borrowings in the seven previous years. The section for the year 425/4 B.C. and the totals for the quadrennium are given below.

The following sums were transmitted by the treasurers Phokiades of Oion´and colleagues, in the archonship of Stratokles and the council (year) for which Pleistias was the first to serve as secretary.

To the generals in the Peloponnese, Demosthenes son of Alkisthenes, of Aphidna, (and colleagues), in the fourth prytany, of (tribe) . . . , third day into the prytany, from the treasury chamber 30 talents; interest thereon was 5910 drachmas.

A second payment, to the generals Nikias son of Nikeratos, of Kydantidai, and colleagues, in the ninth prytany, of (tribe) Pandionis, fifteenth day into the prytany, 100 talents; interest thereon was 2 talents 3800 drachmas.

Sum of expenditure in the term of Phokiades and colleagues, principal, 130 talents; sum of interest on the money spent in the term of Phokiades and colleagues, 3 talents 3710 drachmas . . .

Sum of total expenditure (borrowed) from Athena in the four years from Panathenaia to Panathenaia 747 talents 1253 drachmas. Sum of total interest due Athena in the four years from Panathenaia to Panathenaia 18 talents 3938 drachmas 2 obols.

ATHENIAN DECREE OF FIRST FRUITS TO ELEUSIS,
ca. 422 B.C.
Meiggs-Lewis 73

The council and assembly decree — (the tribe) Kekropis was in prytany, Timoteles was secretary, Kykneas was chairman, the drafting committee submitted the following —

The Athenians shall offer first fruits of their harvests to the two goddesses (Demeter and Persephone), in accordance with ancestral custom and the oracle from Delphi:[21] from every hundred medimnoi[22] of barley not less than 1/6 medimnos and from every hundred medimnoi of wheat not less than 1/12 medimnos; if anyone reaps a harvest of greater, equal or lesser amount, he shall offer first fruits in the same proportion. The demarchs shall collect by demes and shall deliver (their collections) to Eleusis, to the commissioners of sacrifices there. From the funds of the two goddesses three grain pits shall be built at Eleusis according to ancestral custom, wherever the commissioners of sacrifices and the architect think suitable, and they shall store there the harvest that they receive from the demarchs.

The allies shall also offer first fruits in the same way, and the cities shall choose collectors of the harvests in such manner as they decide the grain will best be collected. When it has been collected they shall send it to Athens, and those who bring it shall deliver it to Eleusis, to the commissioners of sacrifices there. If they do not accept it within five days after notice from the deliverers from the city whence the harvest comes, the commissioners of sacrifices shall be fined a thousand drachmas each; and they shall accept from the demarchs also on the same terms.

The council shall choose heralds and send them to the cities to announce the present decree to the assemblies, for the present occasion as soon as possible and in the future whever it thinks best.

The hierophant and the torchbearer at the mysteries shall bid the Greeks offer first fruits of their harvests in accordance with ancestral custom and the oracle from Delphi. (The commissioners) shall record on a tablet the measure of the harvests (received) from the demarchs for each deme and that from the cities for each city, and they shall deposit it in the Eleusinion at Eleusis and in the council chamber.

The council shall send messengers also to all the other Greek cities where in its judgment it is possible, to tell how the Athenians and their allies offer first fruits and, without enjoining it upon them as a duty, to exhort them to offer first fruits if they so desire in accordance with ancestral custom and the oracle from Delphi. The commissioners of sacrifices shall accept on the same terms also from these cities, if any contribute.

They shall sacrifice from the pelanos[23] as the Eumolpids[24] prescribe, and from (the proceeds of) the barley and the wheat an ox-ram-goat triad with gilded horns to each of the two goddesses, an unblemished sheep each to Triptolemos and the god (Hades) and the goddess (Persephone) and Euboulos,[25] and an ox with gilded horns to Athena. The commissioners shall sell the remaining barley and wheat and, together with the council, shall make and dedicate such votive offerings to the two goddesses as the Athenian assembly decrees; and they shall inscribe upon the votive offerings that they were dedicated from the first fruits of the harvests and the names of the Greeks who offered the first fruits. Those who act thus shall have many blessings and good and abundant harvests, whosoever do not wrong the Athenians or the city of Athens or the two goddesses.

Lampon moved –

In addition to the drafting committee's motion concerning the offering of first fruits of the harvests to the two goddesses, the secretary of the council shall inscribe the motion and this decree on two stone stelae and shall place one in the sanctuary at Eleusis and the other on the acropolis. The commissioners shall let the contract for the two stelae, and the kolakretai[26] shall furnish the money.

[A number of technical administrative details follow.]

CONSTRUCTION OF A FOOTBRIDGE VOTED, 421/0 B.C.
Syll. 86

Prepis son of Eupheros was secretary.

The council and assembly decree — (the tribe) Aigeis was in prytany, Prepis was secretary, Patrokles presided, Theaios moved —

to bridge the town-side (branch of the) Rheitos[27] — using stones from the ruins of the old temple at Eleusis[28] which remained unused for the wall — so that the priestesses may carry the sacred statues (in procession) most safely. They shall make the width five feet, so that wagons may not pass through but pedestrians may be able to walk to the ceremonies. They shall cover up the channels of the Rheitos in accordance with the plans of the architect Demomeles. If they are not . . .

[The rest is lost.]

THE ONE-YEAR TRUCE
Thucydides 4.118-119

In 423 B.C., as winter turned toward the spring and a resumption of active hostilities, negotiations were begun — apparently on Sparta's initiative — which quickly led to agreement on a one-year cessation of the Peloponnesian War. Thucydides here reports the Spartan proposals (A), followed by the Athenian decree of ratification (B). A detailed exposition of textual and interpretive matters will be found in A. W. Gomme, *A Historical Commentary on Thucydides,* vol. III (1956), pp. 596 ff.

(A) Concerning the sanctuary and the oracle of Pythian Apollo we agree that anyone who wishes may frequent it without fraud and without fear, in accordance with our ancestral customs. The Spartans and their allies here present[29] so hold, and they promise to the limit of their ability to send heralds to persuade the Boiotians and Phokians. Concerning the treasure of the god we undertake to hunt down the wrongdoers, rightly and justly following our ancestral customs, you and we and those of the others so desiring, all following our ancestral customs. Concerning these matters, then, the Spartans and the others, their allies, are agreed on these terms.

The Spartans and the others, their allies, also agree on the following if the Athenians will make a treaty, that each side will remain on its own territory, holding what we now hold: the (Athenians) remaining in Koryphasion[30] inside Bouphras and Tomeus; those in Kythera[31] having no dealings with the (Spartan) alliance, neither we with them nor they with us; those in Nisaia and Minoa not crossing the road leading from the gates alongside Nisos to the Poseidonion and from the Poseidonion straight to the bridge to Minoa (the Megareans and their allies are also not to cross this road); the Athenians holding the island[32] which they seized, neither side having dealings with the other, and such territory as they now hold in Troizen in accordance with the agreement Troizen made with Athens.

To the extent that they use the sea along the coasts of themselves and their alliance, the Spartans and their allies shall sail not with a warship, but with an oared vessel carrying a burden of up to five hundred talents.

A herald and an embassy and attendants, as many as it seems appropriate (to send) to the Peloponnese and Athens concerning an end to the war and arbitration of disputes, shall enjoy safe-conduct coming and going, both by land and by sea.

Neither you nor we shall receive deserters at this time, neither free nor slave.

You shall give satisfaction to us and we to you according to ancestral custom, settling disputes by arbitration without war.

The Spartans and their allies agree on these conditions. If anything seems to you fairer or juster than these, come to Sparta and demonstrate it: neither the Spartans nor their allies will refuse to consider any proposal that you pronounce just. And let those who come come with power to conclude, just as you bade us. The truce shall be for a year.

* * * * *

(B) The assembly decrees — (the tribe) Akamantis was in prytany, Phainippos was secretary, Nikiades was president (of the prytany), Laches moved —

with the good fortune of the Athenians, to make the armistice on the terms which the Spartans and their allies grant.[33] And they agreed in the assembly that the armistice should be for a year beginning that day, the fourteenth of the month Elapheboli-on;[34] that during that time envoys and heralds should go from each side to the other to discuss on what terms there could be an end to the war; that the generals and prytaneis should summon an assembly for the Athenians to deliberate first of all about peace, on what terms the embassy should offer to end the war; and that forthwith the embassies now present should pledge before the assembly surely to abide by the truce for the year . . .

This, then, was the armistice that came into being, and in the course of it they were continually meeting to talk about a more extensive truce.

THE "PEACE OF NIKIAS"
Thucydides 5.18-19

The first ten years of the Peloponnesian War having proved indecisive, both sides were ready to talk peace, or if not peace, then at least a cessation of all-out warfare. Toward the close of the winter of 422/1 B.C. the terms of peace were agreed upon and ratified. In addition to the treaty with Sparta, a separate, identical treaty was drawn up between Athens (representing also its allies) and each of Sparta's allies, four of which, including Corinth, eventually refused to sign. The treaty was to run for fifty years, but hostilities resumed the very next year, after Athens formed an alliance with three Peloponnesian states, Argos, Mantineia and Elis.

The Athenians and the Spartans and their respective allies have concluded a treaty and sworn to it state by state upon the following terms:

With regard to the common sanctuaries, whoever wishes may offer sacrifices and consult the oracles and attend as a deputy according to the customs of the fathers, both by land and by sea, without fear. The precinct and temple of Apollo at Delphi and the people of Delphi shall be independent, having their own system of taxation and their own courts of justice, both as regards themselves and their own territory, according to the customs of the fathers.

The truce shall be in force for fifty years between the Athenians and their allies and the Spartans and their allies, without fraud or hurt, both by land and by sea. It shall not be lawful to bear arms with harmful intent, either for the Spartans and their allies against the Athenians and their allies, or for the Athenians and their allies against the Spartans and their allies, by any art or device. And if there be any dispute with one another, they shall have recourse to courts and oaths, according as they shall agree.

The Spartans and their allies shall restore Amphipolis to the Athenians. But in the case of cities delivered by the Spartans to the Athenians, their inhabitants shall be allowed to go away wherever they wish, having their own possessions; and these cities, so long as they pay the tribute that was fixed in the time of Aristeides,[35] shall be independent. And it shall not be lawful for the Athenians and their allies, after the ratification of the treaty, to bear arms against the cities to their hurt, so long as they pay the tribute. These cities are Argilos, Stagiros, Akanthos, Stolos, Olynthos, Spartolos. These shall be allies neither of the Spartans nor of the Athenians; but if the Athenians can persuade these cities it shall be lawful for the Athenians to make them, with their own free will and consent, allies to themselves. The Mekybernaians and Sanaians and Singians shall dwell in their own towns on the same terms as the Olynthians and Akanthians.

The Spartans and their allies shall restore Panakton to the Athenians. The Athenians shall restore to the Spartans Koryphasion, Kythera, Methana, Pteleon and Atalante. Also they shall set at liberty the Spartan captives who are in the public prison at Athens or in public prison anywhere else that the Athenians hold sway, and the men of the Peloponnese who are being besieged in Skione, and all besides who are allies of the Spartans in Skione, and those whom Brasidas sent into the place, as likewise any of the allies of the Spartans who are in the public prison at Athens, or in public prison anywhere else that the Athenians have sway. In like manner the Spartans and their allies shall restore whomsoever they have of the Athenians and their allies.[36]

As to Skione, Torone, Sermyle or any other city which the Athenians hold, the Athenians shall determine about these and the other cities as they may think best.[37]

The Athenians shall bind themselves by oaths with the Spartans and their allies, city by city; and either party shall swear its customary oath in the form that is most binding, seventeen men representing each city. The oath shall be as follows: "I will abide by this agreement and this treaty, justly and without deceit." For the Spartans and their allies there shall be an oath, in the same terms, with the Athenians. And both parties shall renew the oath year by year.

They shall erect pillars at Olympia, Delphi, the Isthmus, and on the acropolis at Athens, and at Sparta in the temple of Apollo of Amyklai.

If either party forgets anything about any matter whatsoever, it shall be consistent with their oath for both, by means of fair discussion, to make a change at any point where it may seem good to both parties, the Athenians and the Spartans.

The treaty begins at Sparta in the ephorate of Pleistolas, on the fourth day from the end of the month Artemision, and at Athens in the archonship of Alkaios, on the sixth day from the end of the month Elaphebolion. The following persons took oaths and ratified the treaty: on behalf of the Spartans (17 names), on behalf of the Athenians (17 names).

ATHENS AND SPARTA SIGN AN ALLIANCE, 421 B.C.
Thucydides 5.23-24

Shortly after ratifying the "fifty-years' peace," the same Athenian and Spartan 17-man embassies swore to a treaty of military alliance, the terms of which are here recorded by Thucydides. The following year Athens entered into an alliance "for a hundred years" with Argos, Elis and Mantineia; that treaty, similarly worded but with some additional clauses, is recorded in Thucydides 5.47.

The Spartans and Athenians shall be allies for fifty years on the following conditions:

If any enemy invade the territory of the Spartans and be doing them harm, the Athenians shall help the Spartans in whatever way they can most effectively, with all their might; but if the enemy, after ravaging the country, shall have departed, that city shall be the enemy of the Spartans and Athenians, and shall suffer at the hands of both, and neither city shall make peace with it without the other. These conditions shall be observed honestly, zealously and without fraud.

If any enemy invade the territory of the Athenians and be doing them harm, the Spartans shall help the Athenians in whatever way they can most effectively, with all their might; but if the enemy, after ravaging the country shall have departed, that city shall be the enemy of the Spartans and Athenians, and shall suffer at the hands of both, and neither shall make peace with it without the other. These conditions shall be observed honestly, zealously and without fraud.

If there shall be an insurrection of slaves, the Athenians shall aid the Spartans with all their might, to the utmost of their power.[38]

These articles shall be sworn to by the same persons who swore to the other treaty on both sides. They shall be renewed every year, the Spartans going to Athens at the Dionysia, the Athenians to Sparta at the Hyakinthia. Each party shall erect a pillar, that in Sparta by the temple of Apollo at Amyklai, that at Athens on the acropolis by the temple of Athena.

If it shall seem good to the Spartans and the Athenians to add or take away anything pertaining to the alliance, it shall be consistent with the oaths of both to do whatever may seem good to both.

For the Spartans the following took the oath: (17 names); for the Athenians: (17 names).

EXPENDITURES FOR STATUES
IG 370-71

Statues of Athena and Hephaistos were installed in the temple of the latter, the Hephaistion. Fragments survive from the inscribed accounts of the commissioners for the years 421/0-416/5 B.C. These afford a vivid glimpse of the installation and appearance of such a temple monument.

Gods.

The commissioners in charge of the two statues of the Hephaistion, Apolexis son of Smikythos of Iphistiadai, Chaireas son of Epigonos of Hagnous, Peisandros son of Glauketes of Acharnai, the secretary Oikoteles son of Geisios of Lamptrai. They began the work in the archonship of Aristion, in the council (year) for which Menekles of Anaphlystos was the first to serve as secretary, in the fifth prytany, held by (the tribe) Leontis.

Receipts from the treasurers of the other gods: [There follow, incompletely preserved, the treasurers for the years 420/19-416/5 and the sums received in each year.]

(Expenditures)[39]

Bronze was purchased, 110(?) tal. 10 minas, at 35 dr. per tal.

Tin was purchased for the flower, 1 1/2 tal. 23 1/2 min., at 230 dr. per tal.

Wages for the men fashioning the flower under the shield and the leaves contracted for later

Lead for the flower and for the bonds of the blocks of the pedestal (12 supports).

Wood and charcoal for (melting) the lead.

To the man making the table.

Wage for the man bringing the two statues and erecting them in the temple.

Wood was purchased (1) to make the two ramps on which the two statues were brought in and on which the blocks for the pedestal were brought in, (2) to fence around the pedestal of the two statues and the doors, and (3) to erect scaffolding around the two statues and ramps to the platform.

Sum total of expenditure 5 tal. 3310 dr.

THE TREASURES IN THE HEKATOMPEDOS, 418 B.C.
Meiggs-Lewis 76

Among the records submitted by the treasurers of Athena were annual inventories of the treasures in their care. Most of the treasures accumulated on the acropolis in the course of the fifth century were melted down to provide needed funds in the closing years of the Peloponnesian War. It has been calculated that the objects listed below had a total worth of about ten talents.

The four annual boards (of treasurers) which rendered accounts from Panathenaia to Panathenaia transmitted the following objects in the Hekatompedos shrine to the treasurers Pythodoros of Halai and colleagues, for whom Phormion son of Aristion of Kydathenaion was secretary; and the treasurers for whom Phormion son of Aristion of Kydathenaion was secretary transmitted to the treasurers Anaxikrates of Lamptrai and colleagues, for whom Euxenos son of Euphanes of Prospalta was secretary: 3 gold bowls weighing 2544 dr. A gold statue of a maiden on a stele, no weight record. A silver aspergillum, no weight record. 2 gold crowns weighing 80 dr. A gold crown which the Nike has,[40] weighing 60 dr. 8 silver bowls weighing 400 dr. A silver drinking cup weighing 200 dr. A silver drinking cup of Zeus Polieus weighing 200 dr. A gold crown weighing ... A gold diadem weighing 63 dr. 4 gold crowns weighing 135 dr. 2 ob. A gold crown weighing 18 dr. 3 ob. 2 gold vessels weighing 293 dr. 3 ob. A gold vessel weighing 138 dr. 2 ob. A gold vessel weighing 119 dr. A gold crown weighing 26 dr. 3 ob. A silver vessel weighing 192 dr. A silver censer weighing 1000 dr. During the year were added: A gold crown weighing 1250 dr. A gold crown weighing ... A gold crown weighing 35 dr.

THE ATHENIAN EXPEDITION AGAINST MELOS, 416 B.C.
Tod 76

"Against the island of Melos," wrote Thucydides (5.84.1), "Athens sailed with thirty ships of her own plus six from Chios and two from Lesbos, and with twelve hundred hoplites of her own, three hundred archers and twenty mounted archers, plus some fifteen hundred hoplites from the allies and the islanders." The following fragmentary inscription, found on the acropolis at Athens, shows some correspondence with Thucydides' text and may relate to the expedition against Melos.

[The beginning is broken.]

... they shall select from the Athenians a hundred fifty men by tribes and shall immediately fill thirty troop-transport triremes. They shall man the ships from those chosen by lot. There shall sail in these ships: in each ship five Athenians from the volunteers, and forty hoplites from the draft in each ship by tribes, plus ten archers and fifteen peltasts from the Athenians and the allies. If the generals and trireme-builders do not pay the sailors their wages . . . they shall be fined up to . . .

[The rest is lost.]

SEQUEL TO THE MUTILATION OF THE HERMS
Meiggs-Lewis 79 and Tod 80

One summer's day in 415 B.C. the Athenians awoke to find that over night "most of the stone statues of Hermes in the city — square shaped by local custom, they are numerous both in private doorways and in sacred places — had had their faces mutilated" (Thucydides 6.27.1). Coming on the eve of the much-debated expedition to Sicily, this event was regarded as an act of political subversion as well as a religious offense. Feelings ran so high that, when the property of those condemned for the act was sold (in 414-13 B.C.), the records were inscribed on stone as a permanent public reminder.

Fragments of some ten stelae are extant. Three samples are given below. The left-hand column records the sales tax of roughly one per cent, the next column the sales price.

_ _

3 ob.   18 dr. standing crop at Thria
3 ob.   20 dr. standing crop at Athmonon
Total, including sales taxes, 4723 dr. 5 ob.

(Property of) Polystratos son of Diodoros, of Ankyle:
2 dr. 1 ob.   202 dr. Faithful[41]

1 dr.   42 dr. standing crop at Ankyle
Total, including sales taxes, 247 dr. 1 ob.

(Property of) Kephisodoros, metic in Piraeus:

2 dr.	165 dr.	female Thracian (slave)[42]
1 dr. 3 ob.	135 dr.	female Thracian
2 dr.	170 dr.	male Thracian
2 dr. 3 ob.	240 dr.	male Syrian
1 dr. 3 ob.	105 dr.	male Karian
2 dr.	161 dr.	male Illyrian
2 dr. 3 ob.	220 dr.	female Thracian
1 dr. 3 ob.	115 dr.	male Thracian
1 dr. 3 ob.	144 dr.	male Skythian
1 dr. 3 ob.	121 dr.	male Illyrian
2 dr.	153 dr.	male Kolchian
2 dr.	174 dr.	Karian boy
1 dr.	72 dr.	Karian child
3 dr. 1 ob.	301 dr.	male Syrian
2 dr.	106 dr.	(?fe)male Melitene
1 dr.	85+ dr.	female Lydian

_ _

(Property of) Panaitios:

[lost]	70(?) dr.	104 amphoras 7 choes of pure Attic wine
3 dr.	260 dr.	beehives in the field at Is————————
1 dr. 1 ob.	100 dr.	two female work oxen at Ar————————
[lost]	[lost]	4 cows and —— calves
[lost]	[lost]	84 sheep and their young
7 dr. 3 ob.	710 dr.	67 goats and their young

(Property of) Polystratos son of Diodoros, of Ankyle:

[lost]	[lost]	house in Kydathenaion with a double-folding front door, adjoining the temple of Artemis Amarysia at Athmonon
[lost]	[lost]	property at Ankyle south of the hillock where the temple . . .

_____

(Property of) Alkibiades son of Kleinias, of Skambonidai:[43]

[lost]	two-door chest
[lost]	four-door chest
90 dr.	10 Milesian-work beds
16 dr.	4 tables
17 dr.	low couch, one-armed
11 dr.	plain screen
[lost]	double-ended Milesian-work bed
[lost]	6 perfume jars
[lost]	5 stools
1 dr. 1 ob.	bench
[lost]	2 wicker baskets
[lost]	reed mat

[The fragment lists fifteen more items of clothing and furnishings, their prices lost.]

THE PERSIAN-SPARTAN ALLIANCE, 412 B.C.
Thucydides 8.18, 37 and 58

Athens' disastrous defeat in Sicily started a chain reaction of anti-Athenian diplomatic and military activity. Members of the Confederacy seized this opportunity to secede, protected by Spartan might. The Persian King joined in an anti-Athenian alliance with Sparta, which, in return for his support, allowed him to reassert his sovereignty over the Greek cities of Asia. The alliance was formalized in three successive treaties, the terms of which are recorded by Thucydides.

First Treaty
The Lakedaimonians and their allies have concluded an alliance with the King and Tissaphernes on the following terms:

Whatsoever territory and cities the King holds or the forefathers of the King held, shall belong to the King; and from these cities whatsoever money or anything else came in for the Athenians shall be stopped by the King and the Lakedaimonians and their allies acting in common, to the end that the Athenians shall receive neither money nor anything else.

And the war against the Athenians shall be waged in common by the King and the Lakedaimonians and their allies; and an end of the war against the Athenians is not to be made except with the consent of both parties, the King as well as the Lakedaimonians and their allies.

If any revolt from the King, they shall be enemies to both the Lakedaimonians and their allies, and if any revolt from the Lakedaimonians and their allies, they shall be enemies to the King in like manner.

Second Treaty

Compact of the Lakedaimonians and their allies with King Darius and the King's sons and Tissaphernes. There shall be a treaty and friendship on the following terms:

Whatsoever territory and cities belong to King Darius or belonged to his father or their ancestors, against these shall neither the Lakedaimonians nor their allies go either for war or to do any harm; nor shall either the Lakedaimonians or their allies exact tribute from these cities. Nor shall King Darius or those over whom the King rules go against the Lakedaimonians or their allies for war or to do any harm.

If the Lakedaimonians or their allies have need of anything from the King or the King from the Lakedaimonians or their allies, whatever they shall persuade one another to do, this shall be right for them to do.

The war against the Athenians and their allies both parties shall wage in common; and if they make peace, both shall make it in common.

Whatsoever forces shall be in the territory of the King, on the summons of the King, shall be maintained at the expense of the King.

If any of the cities that have entered into this compact with the King shall go against the country of the King, the rest shall strive to prevent this and aid the King to the extent of their power; and if any of those who inhabit the King's territory or any territory over which the King has dominion shall go against the territory of the Lakedaimonians or of their allies, the King shall strive to prevent this and give aid to the extent of his power.

Third Treaty

In the thirteenth year of the reign of Darius, while Alexippidas was ephor at Sparta, an agreement was made in the plain of the Meander by the Lakedaimonians and their allies with Tissaphernes, Hieramenes, and the sons of Pharnakes respecting the King's affairs and those of the Lakedaimonians and their allies.

The King's country, as much of it as is in Asia, shall be the King's; and concerning his own country the King shall determine as he pleases.

The Lakedaimonians and their allies shall not go against the country of the King to do any harm, nor the King against that of the Lakedaimonians or their allies to do any harm. If any of the Lakedaimonians or their allies shall go with harmful intent against the country of the King, the Lakedaimonians and their allies shall prevent it; and if any from the King's country shall go with harmful intent against the Lakedaimonians or their allies, the King shall prevent it.

Maintenance for the ships now present shall be provided by Tissaphernes according to the compact until the King's ships shall come; and the Lakedaimonians and their allies, after the King's ships arrive, shall be at liberty to maintain their own ships if they so wish. If, however, they desire to receive maintenance from Tissaphernes, he shall furnish it; but the Lakedaimonians and their allies, when the war ends, shall pay back to Tissaphernes whatever money they have received.

And when the ships of the King arrive, the ships of the Lakedaimonians and their allies and those of the King shall wage war in common, according as it may seem best to Tissaphernes and to the Lakedaimonians and their allies. And if they wish to end the war with the Athenians, it shall be ended on the same footing for both.

PUNISHMENT OF ATHENIAN OLIGARCHS
Plutarch, *Lives of the Ten Orators* 1 (*Moralia* 834A-B)

When the oligarchy of the Four Hundred was overthrown in 411 B.C. a decree was passed ordering the arrest, trial and punishment of those who had acted "to the detriment of the city." Under that decree Archeptolemos, one of the Four Hundred, and the orator Antiphon, one of their supporters, were condemned in the following terms. (On the treatise *Lives of the Ten Orators* see p. 47.)

Archeptolemos son of Hippodamos, of (the deme) Agryle, and Antiphon son of Sophilos, of (the deme) Rhamnos, being present (in court) were convicted of treason. The sentence passed upon them was that they be handed over to the Eleven (for execution); that their property be confiscated and a tithe belong to the goddess (Athena); that their houses be razed and on the sites be set boundary stones inscribed "(Property of) Archeptolemos and Antiphon, the traitors"; that their respective demarchs inventory their estates; that it be unlawful to bury Archeptolemos and Antiphon at Athens or anywhere under Athenian control; that Archeptolemos and Antiphon be disfranchised together with their posterity both illegitimate and legitimate, and if anyone adops any descendant of Archeptolemos or Antiphon the adopter shall be disfranchised. This shall be inscribed on a bronze stele and erected where the decrees concerning Phrynichos[44] are set up.

ACCOUNT OF THE TREASURERS OF ATHENA
Meiggs-Lewis 84

A good example of Athenian expenditures during the years of the Peloponnesian War is the following inscription covering the ten prytanies of 410/9 B.C. Most of the unspecified payments were presumably for military purposes.

Athenian expenditures in the archonship of Glaukippos and the council (year) for which Kleigenes of Halai was the first to serve as secretary. The treasurers of the sacred funds of Athena, Kallistratos of Marathon and colleagues, transmitted from the annual accretions on decree of the assembly:

In the first prytany, of (tribe) Aiantis, transmitted to the Hellenotamiai Kallimachos of Hagnous and Phrasitelides of Ikaria, providing fodder for horses, from Athena Polias 3 tal. 3237 dr. 1/2 ob., from (Athena) Nike 91 dr. 3 1/4 ob.

In the second prytany, of (tribe) Aigeis, transmitted to the judges of the games for the Great Panathenaia, to Philon of Kydathenaion and colleagues, from Athena Polias 5 tal. 1000 dr.; to the annual commissioners of rites, Diyllos of Herchia and colleagues, for the sacrifice 5114 dr.

In the third prytany, of (tribe) Oineis, transmitted to the Hellenotamiai Perikles[45] of Cholargos and colleagues, providing fodder for horses, 2 tal. 5420 dr.; item, to the same Hellenotamiai, providing fodder for horses, 2 tal. 5400 dr.; item, to the same Hellenotamiai for Hermon the commandant at Pylos 6 tal.; item, to the same Hellenotamiai for the two-obol fund[46] 2 tal.

In the fourth prytany, of (tribe) Akamantis, transmitted to the Hellenotamiai Perikles of Cholargos and colleagues, providing fodder for horses 3 tal.; item, to the same Hellenotamiai for the two-obol fund, 8 tal. 1355 dr.

In the fifth prytany, of (tribe) Kekropis, transmitted to the Hellenotamiai Perikles of Cholargos and colleagues for the two-obol fund 4 tal. 2200 dr.

In the sixth prytany, of (tribe) Leontis, third day of the prytany, transmitted to the Hellenotamiai Dionysios of Kydathenaion and colleagues 1284 dr.; ninth day of the prytany, to the Hellenotamiai Thrason of Boutadai and colleagues 3 tal. 1083 dr. 2 ob.; eleventh day of the prytany, transmitted to the Helleno-tamiai Proxenos of Aphidna and colleagues, allocation for the general Eukleides from (money collected at) Eretria 3740 dr. 1 1/4 ob.; thirteenth day of the prytany, to the Hellenotamiai Perikles of Cholargos and colleagues 1 tal.(?) 4906 dr.; twenty-eighth day of the prytany, to the Hellenotamiai Spoudias of Phlya and colleagues 2 tal. 2200(?) dr.; thirtieth day of the prytany, the money from Samos allocated to the Hellenotamias Anaitios of Sphettos and his assessor Polyaratos of Cholargos 57 tal. 1000 dr.

In the seventh prytany, of (tribe) Antiochis, fifth day of the prytany, transmitted to Dionysios of Kydathenaion and colleagues for the two-obol fund 1 tal.; seventh day of the prytany, to the Hellenotamiai Thrason of Boutadai and colleagues for the two-obol fund 1 tal. 1232 dr. 3 1/4 ob.; the same day, to the Hellenotamiai Phalanthos of Alopeke and colleagues, fodder for horses 4 tal.; sixteenth day of the prytany, to the Hellenotamiai Proxenos of Aphidna and colleagues, 1534 dr. 3 ob.; twenty-fourth day of the prytany, to the Hellenotamiai Eupolis of Aphidna and colleagues 5400 dr.; twenty-seventh day of the prytany, to the Hellenotamiai Kallias of Euonymon and colleagues 1 tal. 2565 dr. 4 1/2 ob.

In the eighth prytany, of (tribe) Hippothontis, twelfth day of the prytany, transmitted to the Hellenotamiai Proxenos of Aphidna and colleagues 3 tal. 634 dr. 4 ob.; twenty-fourth day of the prytany, given to the Hellenotamiai Dionysios of Kydathenaion and colleagues 3 tal. 4318 dr. 1 1/2 ob.; thirty-sixth day of the prytany, given to the Hellenotamiai Thrason of Boutadai and colleagues 1 tal. 3329 dr. 3 ob.

In the ninth prytany, of (tribe) Erechtheis, twelfth day of the prytany, given to the Hellenotamiai Proxenos of Aphidna and colleagues 3188(?) dr. 1 ob.; twenty-third day of the prytany, given to the Hellenotamiai Dionysios of Kydathenaion and colleagues 4(?) tal. 793 dr. 3 ob.; thirty-sixth day of the prytany, given to the Hellenotamiai Thrason of Boutadai and colleagues 2 tal. 3850 dr. 2 1/2 ob.; thirty-sixth day of the prytany, the allies allocated the money from Samos to the generals at Samos — to Dexikrates of Aigilia 21 tal. 1000 dr., to Pasiphon of Phrearrhioi 6 tal., to Aristokrates of [lost] 5 tal., to [lost] of Euonymon 5 tal. 3896 dr., to Nikeratos[47] of Kydantidai, the trierarch, 3000 dr., to Aristophanes of Anaphlystos, the trierarch, [amount lost].

In the tenth prytany, of (tribe) Pandionis, eleventh day of the prytany, given to the Hellenotamiai Proxenos of Aphidna and colleagues 5 tal. 442 dr. 5 ob.; twenty-third day of the prytany, given to the Hellenotamiai [names lost] and colleagues 2 tal. 5090 dr. 3 ob.; thirty-sixth day of the prytany, given to the Hellenotamiai [names lost] and colleagues 5 tal. 4656 dr. 4 ob.

Sum total of money which Kallistratos of Marathon and colleagues transmitted . . . [the rest is lost.][48]

ERECHTHEION CONSTRUCTION RECORDS
IG 372

In this progress report the supervisory commissioners of 409/8 B.C. detail the state of the stone work for the Erechtheion as they found it when they took office. The items listed and described make it clear that the Erechtheion was then nearing completion.

The captions and representative samples of the details of this long inscription are given below.

The commissioners in charge of the temple on the acropolis housing the ancient statue, Brosynides of Kephisia, Chariades of Agryle, Diodes of Kephisia, the architect Philokles of Acharnai and the secretary Etearchos of Kydathenaion, in accordance with the decree of the assembly moved by Epigenes inscribed (this record of) the work of the temple as they found it, finished and unfinished,[49] in the archonship of Diokles, in the first prytany, held by (the tribe) Kekropis, in the council (year) for which Nikophanes of Marathon was the first to serve as secretary.

We found the following work of the temple unfinished

At the corner toward the Kekropion:[50] 4 blocks not in place, 4 ft. long, 2 ft. wide, 1 1/2 ft. thick; 1 cornerstone 4 ft. long, 3 ft. wide, 1 1/2 ft. thick; 5 top-course blocks 4 ft. long, 3 ft. wide, 1 1/2 ft. thick; 1 angle stone 7 ft. long, 4 ft. wide, 1 1/2 ft. thick; 1 round stone not in place, corresponding with the top-course blocks, 10 ft. long, 1 1/2 ft. high; 2 blocks corresponding with the architraves, 4 ft. long, 5 palms wide; 1 column capital not in place and the inner face, 2 ft. long, 1 1/2 ft. wide, 1 1/2 ft. thick; 5 architraves not in place, 8 ft. long, 2 ft. 1 palm wide, 2 ft. thick; 3 architraves in place but still to be dressed, 8 ft. long, 2 ft. 1 palm wide, 2 ft. thick . . .

At the porch[51] toward the Kekropion: Needed, to dress the roof stones over the Maidens on top, 13 ft. long, 5 ft. wide. To dress the rosettes on the architraves needed.

Stone work completely finished but still on the ground: 11 blocks 4 ft. long, 2 ft. wide, 1 1/2 ft. thick; 1 cornerstone 4 ft. long, 3 ft. wide, 1 1/2 ft. thick . . .

Of each of the following the second joint has not been finished, nor the back joints: 12 blocks 6 ft. long, 2 ft. wide, 1 ft. thick — of each of these the second joint has not been finished, nor the back joints; 5 blocks 4 ft. long, 2 ft. wide, 1 ft. thick — of each of these the second joint has not been finished, nor the back joints; 1 block 5 ft. long, 2 ft. wide, 1 ft. thick — of this the second joint is not begun, nor the back joints.

Cornice stones 4 ft. long, 3 ft. wide, 5 palms thick: 7 finished smooth, without carving; 5 others, same size, 4 ft. of volute and moulding of each were uncarved; of 2 others 4 ft. of the volute and 8 ft. of the moulding were uncarved . . .

On the wall toward the Pandroseion:[52] 1 block 7 1/2 ft. long, 3 1/2 ft. wide — the smoothing unfinished; 1 block 6 ft. long, 3 ft. 1 palm wide, 5 palms thick, on the wall toward the Pandroseion — of this 5 ft. of moulding uncarved; 6 pediment stones from the stoa, 7 ft. long, 3 1/2 ft. wide, 1 ft. thick — these are unfinished; 2 others 5 ft. long, 3 1/2 ft. wide, 1 ft. thick — unfinished . . .

4 stone doors 8 ft. 1 palm long, 2 1/2 ft. wide — of these the rest had been finished but the black stones[53] were still to be set into the panels; 1 side ornament for the east lintel — unfinished; Pentelic marble for the altar of the sacrificing priest, 3 blocks 4 ft. long, 2 ft. 1 palm high, 1 ft. thick, another 3 ft. long . . .

THE VICTORY OF LYSANDER
Fouilles de Delphes vol. III 1, no. 50

Two marble fragments found in the excavation at Delphi in 1894 proved to be the base of a statue erected there by Lysander to commemorate his victory over the Athenians at Aigispotamoi in 405 B.C. The pedestal bears the following inscription in two elegiac couplets and a signature.

Lysander dedicated his statue on this base when in the triumph of his swift ships he destroyed the might of the Kekro pidai,[54] thus crowning unravaged Sparta, the citadel of Hellas, his fatherland of the beautiful dance grounds.

Ion of sea-girt Samos fashioned this elegiac poem.

ATHENS REWARDS THE SAMIANS
Meiggs-Lewis 94

In the general defection of unwilling allies that followed the disaster at Aigispotamoi, Samos alone remained loyal to Athens. Fearing that the Spartan victory might trigger an oligarchic putsch, the Samians put to death a number of their oligarchs and sent embassies to assure Athens of their continued loyalty. The Athenians thereupon passed the following measures, granting the Samians two gifts that Athens rarely bestowed: Athenian citizenship and local autonomy. The date is 405/4 B.C.

Kephisophon of Paiania was secretary.

For all the Samians who sided with the Athenian government.

The council and assembly decree — (the tribe) Kekropis was in prytany, Polymnis of Euonymon was secretary, Alexias was archon, Nikophon of Athmonon presided; on motion of Kleisophos and co-prytaneis[55] —

We commend the Samian envoys, both those coming previously and those now, and the council and generals and other Samians because they are worthy men and zealous to work whatever good they can, and because we deem that in acting as they did they served the security of Athens and Samos. In return for the benefits they have conferred upon the Athenians and the important new ones they now propose, the council and assembly decree:

that the Samians shall be Athenians, and shall govern themselves however they themselves may wish; and that, to render these provisions as advantageous as possible to both parties, we shall — as they themselves propose — consult in common concerning other details when peace comes; and

that they shall live under their own laws and be autonomous, and shall act in all other matters in accordance with the treaties and covenants, exactly as agreed by Athens and Samos;[56] and that in any claims that may arise against each other they shall give and receive justice in accordance with the existing guarantees; and

that if even before (the peace) any necessity arises from the war regarding the government we shall — as the envoys themselves propose — take counsel and action pro tem in whatever way appears to be best; and that regarding the peace, if it comes, the same conditons shall prevail as exist for the Athenians and for the present inhabitants of Samos; and that if it is necessary to wage war they shall prepare themselves to the best of their ability, acting in concert with the (Athenian) generals; and that if the Athenians send an embassy anywhere, those present from Samos shall send someone along if they wish, and they shall offer whatever good counsel they have; and

that we shall give them the triremes now at Samos to equip and use as seems best to them; and that the (Samian) envoys shall register with the secretary of the council and with the generals the names of the trierarchs whose ships these were, and if ever a judgment for debt is entered in the public archive against these (trierarchs) because they had accepted responsibility for the triremes, the superintendents of the dockyards shall expunge all such records from every source, but they shall return the (triremes') gear to the state as quickly as possible and shall compel those holding any such to return it intact.

On motion of Kleisophos and co-prytaneis —

In addition to all else as proposed by the council, those of the Samians coming (on the embassy) shall — in accordance with their own request — have citizenship (at once), and shall be distributed among the demes and the ten tribes; and the generals shall see to the envoys' (return) journey as quickly as possible; and we commend Eumachos and all the other Samians coming with him as being worthy men towards the Athenians; and we invite Eumachos to dinner in the prytaneion tomorrow.[57]

The secretary of the council together with the generals shall inscribe these provisions on a stone stele and erect it on the acropolis, and the Hellenotamiai shall furnish the money;[58] and they shall inscribe it at Samos in the same way at their own expense.

OUSTER OF THE THIRTY
AND RESTORATION OF DEMOCRACY AT ATHENS, 403 B.C.
A. Aristotle, *Constitution of Athens* 39
B. Andocides, *Oration* 1, §§ 83-84
C. *Ibid.*, 96-98

The archonship of Eukleides, 403/2 B.C., marks a milestone in Athenian history. The oligarchic government of the Thirty, installed at Athens in the summer of 404 B.C. under the protection of the Spartan garrison, launched a reign of terror that led half a year later to its ouster by a band of exiled democrats. The survivors of the Thirty agreed to relinquish Athens in exchange for a safe-conduct to Eleusis (where they met death a few years later). This agreement is given in A, below. Sixty years later the orator Aischines remarked (*Oration* 2, §176), "When the exiled democracy returned ... its leaders imposed an oath on both parties to forgive and forget, for which all judged our city to be very wise, and thereupon the city enjoyed a new beginning of life and power." Five hundred years later that story was still being told with appreciation, as we see in the *Description of Greece* (1.29.3) of Pausanias, "the ancient Baedeker": coming to the tomb of Thrasyboulos outside Athens, he writes, "He ended the tyranny of those called the Thirty, starting out from Thebes with sixty men, and he induced the warring Athenians to come to terms with one another and to abide by their agreement."

Soon after the withdrawal of the Thirty, the reestablished democracy created a commission of nomothetai to revise and update the laws (B), and one of the laws of the "codification" imposed the sanctions of death and confiscation against any future attempt to overthrow the democratic form of government (C).

Another step toward "modernization" taken by Athens in the same year of reform was the abandonment of the old Attic alphabet in favor of the more prevalent Ionic letters.

A

The agreement was made in the archonship of Eukleides, on the following terms:

"Those of the Athenians who remained in the city (under the Thirty) desiring to do so shall be allowed to emigrate to Eleusis, remaining citizens, being sovereign and self-governing, and enjoying their own revenues. The sanctuary shall be common to both parties, and the Kerykes and Eumolpidai shall superintend it in accordance with ancestral custom. It shall be unlawful for those at Eleusis to go to the city or those in the city to Eleusis, except for both at the (celebration of the) mysteries. They shall contribute from their revenues to the common defense fund just like the other Athenians. If any of the emigrés take a house at Eleusis, they must have the consent of the owner; if they do not come to terms with each other, each shall choose three assessors and shall accept whatever price these fix. Those of the Eleusinians may (continue to) dwell there whom these (new settlers) are willing to accept. The registration of those wishing to emigrate shall take place, for those in Attica within ten days of the swearing of the oath (of peace), and their departure within twenty days, and for those outside the country in the same way when they return. It shall be unlawful for an inhabitant of Eleusis to hold any of the magistracies in the city before registering again as an inhabitant of the city. Trials for homicide shall take place in accordance with ancestral custom if a man strikes and kills another with his own hand. For bygones it shall be unlawful for anyone to prosecute anyone except the Thirty, the Ten, the Eleven and the former governors of the Peiraieus,[59] and not even these if they render their accounts; the former governors in Peiraieus shall render accounts before the reviewers in Peiraieus, and those in the city before a panel of property owners, and on these terms those so desiring may emigrate. Each party shall pay back separately the loans which it contracted for the (civil) war."

B[60]

The assembly decrees, on motion of Teisamenos —

that the Athenians shall govern themselves in accordance with ancestral custom, observing the laws, measures and weights of Solon, and observing the ordinances of Drakon, which we observed in former times. Those nomothetai chosen by the council shall inscribe on tablets (these and?) any additions needed and shall display them in public by the eponymoi,[61] for anyone so desiring to examine, and they shall transmit them to the magistrates in this month. The laws being transmitted shall be scrutinized first by the council and the five hundred nomothetai elected by the demes, after they have sworn their oath; and any private citizen so desiring shall be allowed to come before the council to offer any good counsel he may have regarding the laws. When the laws have been ratified, the Council of the Areiopagos shall supervise the laws, to the end that the magistracies may apply (only) the established laws. And they shall inscribe those of the laws that are valid on the wall where they were formerly inscribed, for anyone so desiring to examine.

C

The council and the assembly decree — (the tribe) Aiantis was in prytany, Kleigenes was secretary, Boethos was president, Demophantos and colleagues moved —

. . . If anyone undoes the democracy at Athens or holds any office after the democracy has been undone, he shall be an enemy of the Athenians and may be slain with impunity, and his property shall be confiscated, a tenth to the goddess. The killer of anyone so doing and the accomplice (of the killer) shall be (regarded as) pious and guiltless. All Athenians shall swear by tribes and demes over unblemished sacrificial victims to kill anyone so doing. The oath shall be: "By word and deed and vote and my own hand I will kill, if I can, whoever undoes the democracy at Athens, as well as anyone who thereafter holds any office after the democracy has been undone and anyone who rises up to be a tyrant or who helps establish the tyrant. If someone else kills (such), I will regard him as pious before gods and divinities, as having slain an enemy of the Athenians, and I will sell all the property of the one killed and turn over half to the killer, withholding nothing. If someone is slain in killing someone of these or in the attempt, I will treat him and his children just like Harmodios and Aristogeiton and their offspring. All oaths sworn at Athens or in the army or anywhere else in opposition to democratic government at Athens[62] I annul and invalidate." This lawful oath shall all Athenians swear over unblemished sacrificial victims before the Dionysia; and they shall pray for blessings for him who abides by the oath, and destruction to himself and his house for him who breaks the oath.

REWARD FOR HELPING TO OVERTHROW
THE THIRTY TYRANTS
Syll. 120

The beginning of the end for the Thirty Tyrants came in December 404 B.C., when 70 men led by Thrasyboulos seized Phyle, a stronghold on Mt. Parnes. Volunteers streaming in soon raised the number to 1,000. With this force Thrasyboulos occupied the Mounychia promontory in the Peiraieus. There many aliens joined the ranks on the promise that they would be given citizen status. In 401/0 B.C. the promise was made good with the passage of the following decree.

Lysiades was secretary, Xenainetos was archon.

The council and assembly decree — _____ was in prytany, Lysiades was secretary, Demophilos presided, _____ moved —

that the metics who came back with (the party) from Phyle partake of the same benefaction as those of the citizens who came back . . . was voted by the Athenians. They and their descendants shall have citizenship, enrolled in whatever tribe and deme and phratry they wish, and the magistracies shall apply the same laws to them as to the Athenians, because . . . they fought together (with the Athenians) the battle at Mounychia, they . . . when the reconciliation took place and they carried out their orders . . .

[The rest of the decree is lost. On another fragment there is the following list of the persons to whom the decree applied.]

Chairedemos, farmer	Bendiphanes, digger(?)
Leptines, butcher	Emporion, farmer
Demetrios, carpenter	Paidikos, baker
Euphorion, muleteer	Sosias, fuller
Kephisodoros, builder	Psammis, farmer
Hegesias, gardener	Egersis (no entry)
Epameinon, donkey driver	[one name lost]
[one name lost]	Eukolion, hireling
Glaukias, farmer	Kallias, statue maker
[one name lost]	[one name lost]
Dionysios, farmer	(Tribe) Aigeis
[(Tribe) Erechtheis]	Athenogiton

[A few names can be read in a third column.]

A PROSPEROUS ATHENIAN METIC
[Plutarch], *Lives of the Ten Orators* 3 (*Moralia* 835C-836A)

Falsely attributed to Plutarch in the manuscripts of his *Moralia*, this little treatise on the "canonical" Greek orators is nevertheless replete with interesting anecdote and valuable detail about classical Athens.

Lysias was the son of Kephalos, grandson of Lysanias, and great-grandson of Kephalos. His father was by birth a Syracusan but moved to Athens because he wished to live in that city and also because Perikles, son of Xanthippos, persuaded him to do so, as he was a personal friend of Perikles and they were connected by ties of hospitality, and he was a man of great wealth. But some say that he moved because he was banished from Syracuse when Gelon was tyrant. Lysias was born at Athens in the archonship of the Philokles who succeeded Phrasikles, in the second year of the eightieth Olympiad, and at first he was a schoolmate of the most prominent Athenians; but when the city sent the colony to Sybaris, which was afterwards renamed Thourioi, he went out with his eldest brother Polemarchos (for he had two others, Euthydemos and Brachyllos), their father being already dead, to share in the allotment of land. This was in the archonship of Praxiteles, and he was then fifteen years old. He remained there, was instructed by the Syracusans Teisias and Nikias, acquired a house, had a share of the allotment, and was a citizen for thirty-three years, until Kleokritos was archon at Athens. But in the next year, when Kallias was archon, in the ninety-second Olympiad, when the misfortunes in Sicily had happened to the Athenians and unrest had arisen among the allies in general and especially those who dwelt in Italy, he was accused of favoring Athens and, with three hundred others, was banished. Arriving at Athens in the archonship of the Kallias who succeeded Kleokritos, when the Four Hundred already had possession of the city, he remained there. But when the battle of Aigispotamoi had taken place and the Thirty had taken possession of the city, he was banished after having been there seven years. He was deprived of his property and lost his brother Polemarchos, but he himself escaped from the house in which he was kept to be executed (for it had two doors) and lived at Megara. But when the men at Phyle set about their return to Athens, he was seen to be more helpful than anyone else, since he supplied two thousand drachmas and two hundred shields and, when sent with Hermas, hired three hundred mercenaries and persuaded Thrasydaios of Elis, who had become his guest-friend, to give two talents. For these services Thrasyboulos, after the restoration of the exiles to the city and in the period of anarchy before Eukleides, proposed a grant of citizenship for him, and the popular assembly ratified the grant, but when Archinos had him up for illegality because it had not been previously voted by the council, the enactment was declared void. And after losing his citizenship in this way, he lived the rest of his life at Athens with all the rights of citizenship except the vote and eligibility to office, and died there at the age of eighty-three years or, as some say, seventy-six or, as others say, over eighty; and he lived to see Demosthenes as a youth. They say he was born in the archonship of Philokles.

Four hundred and twenty-five orations attributed to him are current. Of these Dionysios and Caecilius and their school say that two hundred and thirty-three are genuine, and he is said to have lost his case with only two of them. There is also his speech in support of the enactment against which Archinos brought suit and deprived him of citizenship, and another against the Thirty. He was very persuasive and concise and produced most of his speeches for private clients. There are also Textbooks of Rhetoric prepared by him, and Public Addresses, Letters and Eulogies, Funeral Speeches, Love Speeches, and a Defense of Socrates addressed to the judges. In the matter of his diction he appears to be easy, although in fact he is hard to imitate. Demosthenes in his speech against Neaira says that he was in love with Metaneira, a fellow-slave with Neaira; but later he married the daughter of his brother Brachyllos. Plato also mentions him in the *Phaedrus* as an able speaker and older than Isocrates.

ATHENS IDEALIZED
Isocrates, *Panegyrikos* § § 103-106, 115-120

Composed ca. 380 B.C., the *Panegyrikos* is a tract urging the Greek cities to unite (against Persian resurgence) under Athenian leadership, which Isocrates justifies — in contrast to Spartan repression and ineptitude — by picturing the period of the Delian Confederacy as one of enlightened rule and a bringer of benefits to Athens' adherents. In passing it may be noted that Isocrates returned to this theme in his *Panathenaikos*, which he composed toward the end of his long life (339 B.C.), when the domination of Philip of Macedon over the Greek cities was all but achieved.

But I believe that all men are of the opinion that those will prove the best leaders and champions of the Hellenes under whom in the past those who yielded obedience have fared the best. Well, then, it will be found that under our supremacy the private households grew most prosperous and that the commonwealths also became greatest. For we were not jealous of the growing states, nor did we engender confusion among them by setting up conflicting polities side by side, in order that faction might be arrayed against faction and that both might court our favor. On the contrary, we regarded harmony among our allies as the common boon of all, and therefore we governed all the cities under the same laws, deliberating about them in the spirit of allies, not of masters; guarding the interests of the whole confederacy but leaving each member of it free to direct its own affairs; supporting the people but making war on despotic powers, considering it an outrage that the many should be subject to the few, that those who were poorer in fortune but not inferior in other respects should be banished from the offices, that, further-more, in a fatherland which belongs to all in common some should hold the place of masters, others of aliens, and that men who are citizens by birth should be robbed by law of their share in the government.

It was because we had these objections, and others besides, to oligarchies that we established the same polity in the other states as in Athens itself — a polity which I see no need to extol at greater length, since I can tell the truth about it in a word: They continued to live under this regime for seventy years, and, during this time, they experienced no tyrannies, they were free from the domination of the barbarians, they were untroubled by internal factions, and they were at peace with all the world. . .

And, furthermore, not even the present peace, nor yet that "autonomy" which is inscribed in the treaties but is not found in our governments, is preferable to the rule of Athens. For who would desire a condition of things where pirates command the seas and mercenaries occupy our cities; where fellow-countrymen, instead of waging war in defence of their territories against strangers, are fighting within their own walls against each other; where more cities have been captured in war than before we made the peace; and where revolutions follow so thickly upon each other that those who are at home in their own countries are more dejected than those who have been punished with exile? For the former are in dread of what is to come, while the latter live ever in the hope of their return. And so far are the states removed from "freedom" and "autonomy" that some of them are ruled by tyrants, some are controlled by alien governors, some have been sacked and razed, and some have become slaves to the barbarians — the same barbarians whom we once so chastened for their temerity in crossing over into Europe, and for their overweening pride, that they not only ceased from making expeditions against us, but even endured to see their own territory laid waste; and we brought their power so low, for all that they had once sailed the sea with twelve hundred ships, that they launched no ship of war this side of Phaselis but remained inactive and waited on more favorable times rather than trust in the forces which they then possessed.

And that this state of affairs was due to the valor of our ancestors has been clearly shown in the fortunes of our city; for the very moment when we were deprived of our dominion marked the beginning of a dominion of ills for the Hellenes. In fact, after the disaster which befell us in the Hellespont, when our rivals took our place as leaders, the barbarians won a naval victory, became rulers of the sea, occupied most of the islands, made a landing in Lakonia, took Kythera by storm, and sailed around the whole Peloponnesos, inflicting damage as they went.

One may best comprehend how great is the reversal in our circumstances if he will read side by side the treaties which were made during our leadership and those which have been published recently; for he will find that in those days we were constantly setting limits to the empire of the King, levying tribute on some of his subjects, and barring him from the sea; now, however, it is he who controls the destinies of the Hellenes, who dictates what they must each do, and who all but sets up his viceroys in their cities.

ATHENS DESPISED
Anonymous, *Constitution of Athens*

In the introduction to his edition G. W. Bowersock writes, "The treatise is among the most enigmatic and most important of the literary texts from classical Greece. The author has never been identified, and probably cannot be" (Xenophon vol. VII, Loeb Classical Library, 1968, p. 462). Attributed in the manuscripts to "Xenophon the orator," the treatise is clearly the product of a man of strong pro-oligarchic, anti-democratic views and sentiments — "The Old Oligarch," as one modern writer has dubbed him. Attempts to date the treatise from internal evidence have resulted in a scholarly dispute that has continued for over a hundred years. The dates proposed fall in the period between 443 and 415 B.C. The principal arguments are summarized by Bowersock, *op. cit.*, pp. 463-65.

Now, as concerning the constitution of the Athenians, and the type or manner of constitution which they have chosen, I praise it not, in so far as the very choice involves the welfare of the baser folk as opposed to that of the better class. I repeat, I withhold my praise so far; but, given the fact that this is the type agreed upon, I propose to show that they set about its preservation in the right way; and that those other transactions in connection with it, which are looked upon as blunders by the rest of the Hellenic world, are the reverse.

In the first place, I maintain, it is only just that the poorer classes and the people of Athens should be better off than the men of birth and wealth, seeing that it is the people who man the fleet, and put round the city her girdle of power. The steersman, the boatswain, the commandant, the lookout-man at the prow, the shipwright — these are the ones who engird the city with power rather than her heavy infantry and men of birth and quality. This being the case, it seems only just that offices of state should be thrown open to every one both in the ballot and the show of hands, and that the right of speech should belong to any one who likes, without restriction. For observe, there are many of these offices which, according as they are in good or in bad hands, are a source of safety or of danger to the people, and in these the people prudently abstains from sharing; as, for instance, it does not think it incumbent on itself to share in the functions of the general or of the commander of cavalry. The sovereign people recognizes the fact that in forgoing the personal exercise of these offices, and leaving them to the control of the more powerful citizens, it secures the balance of advantage to itself. It is only those departments of government which bring emolument and assist the private estate that the people cares to keep in its own hands.

In the next place, in regard to what some people are puzzled to explain — the fact that everywhere greater consideration is shown to the base, to poor people and to common folk, than to persons of good quality — so far from being a matter of surprise, this, as can be shown, is the keystone of the preservation of the democracy. It is these poor people, this common fold, this riff-raff, whose prosperity, combined with the growth of their numbers, enhances the democracy whereas a shifting of fortune to the advantage of the wealthy and the better classes implies the establishment on the part of the commonalty of a strong power in opposition to itself. In fact, all the world over, the cream of society is in opposition to the democracy. Naturally, since the smallest amount of intemperance and injustice, together with the highest scrupulousness in the pursuit of excellence, is to be found in the ranks of the better class, while within the ranks of the people will be found the greatest amount of ignorance, disorderliness, rascality — poverty acting as a stronger incentive to base conduct, not to speak of lack of education and ignorance, traceable to the lack of means which afflicts the average of mankind.

The objection may be raised that it was a mistake to allow the universal right of speech and a seat in council. These should have been reserved for the cleverest, the flower of the community. But here, again, it will be found that they are acting with wise deliberation in granting to even the baser sort the right of speech, for supposing only the better people might speak or sit in council, blessings would fall to the lot of those like themselves, but to the commonalty the reverse of blessings. Whereas now, any one who likes, any base fellow, may get up and discover something to the advantage of himself and his equals. It may be retorted: "And what sort of advantage either for himself or for the people can such a fellow be expected to hit upon? " The answer to which is, that in their judgment the ignorance and the baseness of this fellow, together with his goodwill, are worth a great deal more to them than your superior person's virtue and wisdom, coupled with animosity. What it comes to, therefore, is that a state founded upon such institutions will not be the best state; but, given a democracy, these are the right means to secure its preservation. The people, it must be borne in mind, does not demand that the city should be well governed and itself a slave. It desires to be free and to be master. As to bad legislation it does not concern itself about that. In fact, what you believe to be bad legislation is the very source of the people's strength and freedom. But if you seek for good legislation, in the first place you will see the cleverest members of the community laying down the laws for the rest. And in the next place, the better class will curb and chastise the lower orders; the better class will deliberate in behalf of the state, and not suffer crack-brained fellows to sit in council, or to speak or vote in the assembly. No doubt; but under the weight of such blessings the people will in a very short time be reduced to slavery.

Another point is the extraordinary amount of license granted to slaves and resident aliens at Athens, where a blow is illegal, and a slave will not step aside to let you pass him in the street. I will explain the reason of this peculiar custom. Supposing it were legal for a slave to be beaten by a free citizen, or for a resident alien or freedman to be beaten by a citizen, it would frequently happen that an Athenian might be mistaken for a slave or an alien and receive a beating; since the Athenian people is not better clothed than the slave or alien, nor in personal appearance is there any superiority. Or if the fact itself that slaves in Athens are allowed to indulge in luxury, and indeed in some cases to live magnificently, be found astonishing, this too, it can be shown, is done of set purpose. Where you have a naval power dependent upon wealth we must perforce be slaves to our slaves, in order that we may get

in our slave-rents and let the real slave go free. Where you have
wealthy slaves it ceases to be advantageous that my slave should
stand in awe of you. In Sparta my slave stands in awe of you. But
if your slave is in awe of me there will be a risk of his giving away
his own moneys to avoid running a risk in his own person. It is for
this reason then that we have established an equality between our
slaves and free men; and again between our resident aliens and full
citizens, because the city stands in need of her resident aliens to
meet the requirements of such a multiplicity of arts and for the
purposes of her navy. That is, I repeat, the justification of the
equality conferred upon our resident aliens.

Citizens devoting their time to gymnastics and to the cultivation of music are not to be found in Athens; the sovereign people
has disestablished them, not from any disbelief in the beauty and
honor of such training, but recognizing the fact that these are
things the cultivation of which is beyond its power. On the same
principle, in the case of the choregia, the gymnasiarchy, and the
trierarchy, the fact is recognised that it is the rich man who trains
the chorus, and the people for whom the chorus is trained; it is the
rich man who is trierarch or gymnasiarch, and the people that
profits by their labours. In fact, what the people looks upon as its
right is to pocket the money. To sing and run and dance and man
the vessels is well enough, but only in order that the people may
be the gainer, while the rich are made poorer. And so in the courts
of justice, justice is not more an object of concern to the jurymen
than what touches personal advantage.

To speak next of the allies, and in reference to the point that
emissaries from Athens come out and, according to common
opinion, calumniate and vent their hatred upon the better sort of
people, this is done on the principle that the ruler cannot help
being hated by those whom he rules; but that if wealth and
respectability are to wield power in the subject cities the empire of
the Athenian people has but a short lease of existence. This
explains why the better people are punished with infamy, robbed
of their money, driven from their homes, and put to death, while
the baser sort are promoted to honor. On the other hand, the
better Athenians throw their aegis over the better class in the
allied cities. And why? Because they recognise that it is to the
interest of their own class at all times to protect the best element

in the cities. It may be urged that if it comes to strength and power the real strength of Athens lies in the capacity of her allies to contribute their money quota. But to the democratic mind it appears a higher advantage still for the individual Athenian to get hold of the wealth of the allies, leaving them only enough to live upon and to cultivate their estates, but powerless to harbor treacherous designs.

Again, it is looked upon as a mistaken policy on the part of the Athenian democracy to compel her allies to voyage to Athens in order to have their cases tried. On the contrary, it is easy to reckon up what a number of advantages the Athenian people derives from the practice. In the first place, they draw pay throughout the year from the court fees. Next, they manage the affairs of the allied states while seated at home without the expense of naval expeditions. Thirdly, they thus preserve the partisans of the democracy, and ruin her opponents in the law courts. Whereas, supposing the several allied states tried their cases at home, being inspired by hostility to Athens they would destroy those of their own citizens whose friendship to the Athenian people was most marked. But besides all this the democracy derives the following advantages from hearing the cases of her allies in Athens. In the first place, the one per cent levied in Peiraieus is increased to the profit of the state; again, the owner of a lodging-house does better, and so, too, the owner of a pair of beasts, or of slaves to be let out on hire; again, heralds and criers are a class of people who fare better owing to the sojourn of foreigners at Athens. Further still, supposing the allies did not have to resort to Athens for the hearing of cases, only the official representatives of Athens would be held in honor, such as the general or trierarch or ambassador. Whereas now every single individual among the allies is forced to flatter the people of Athens because he knows that he must betake himself to Athens and win or lose his case at the bar of none other than the people, which is the law at Athens. He is compelled to behave as a suppliant in the courts of justice, and when some juryman comes into court, to grasp his hand. For this reason, therefore, the allies find themselves more and more in the position of slaves to the people of Athens.

Furthermore, owing to the possession of property beyond the limits of Attika and the exercise of magistracies which take them into regions beyond the frontier, they and their attendants have unconsciously acquired the art of oarsmanship. A man who is perpetually voyaging is forced to handle the oar, he and his domestic alike, and to learn the terms familiar in seamanship. Hence a stock of skilful mariners is produced, bred upon a wide experience of voyaging and practice. They have learnt their business, some in piloting a small craft, others a merchant vessel, while others have been drafted off from these for service on a ship-of-war. So that the majority of them are able to row the moment they set foot on board a vessel, having been in a state of preliminary practice all their lives.

As to the heavy infantry, the deficiency of which at Athens is well recognized, this is how the matter stands. They recognize the fact that, in reference to the hostile power, they are themselves inferior, and must be even if their heavy infantry were more numerous. But relatively to the allies, who bring in the tribute, their strength even on land is enormous. And they are persuaded that their heavy infantry is sufficient for all purposes, provided they retain this superiority. Apart from all else, to a certain extent fortune must be held responsible for the actual condition. The subjects of a power which is dominant by land have it open to them to form contingents from several small states and to muster in force for battle. But with the subjects of a naval power it is different. Inasmuch as they are groups of islanders it is impossible for their states to meet together for united action, for the sea lies between them, and the dominant power is master of the sea. And even if it were possible for them to assemble in some single island unobserved, they would only do so to perish by famine. And as to the states subject to Athens which are not islanders, but situated on the continent, the larger are held in check by need and the small ones absolutely by fear, since there is no state in existence which does not depend upon imports and exports, and these she will forfeit if she does not lend a willing ear to those who are masters by sea. In the next place, a power dominant by sea can do certain things which a land power is debarred from doing; as, for instance, ravage the territory of a superior, since it is always possible to coast along to some point, where either there is no hostile force to deal with or merely a small body; and in case of an advance in force on the part of the enemy they can take to their ships and sail away. Such a performance is attended with less difficulty than that experienced by the relieving force on land. Again, it is open to a power so dominating by sea to leave its own territory and sail off on as long a voyage as you please. Whereas the land power cannot place more than a few days' journey between itself and its own territory, for marches are slow affairs, and it is not possible for any army on the march to have food supplies to last for any great length of time. Such an army must either march through friendly territory or it must force a way by victory in battle. The voyager meanwhile has it in his power to disembark at any point where he finds himself in superior force, or, at the worst, to coast by until he reaches either a friendly district or an enemy too weak to resist. Again, those diseases to which the fruits of the earth are liable as visitations from heaven fall severely on a land power, but are scarcely felt by the naval power; for such sicknesses do not visit the whole earth everywhere at once, so that the ruler of the sea can get in supplies from a thriving district. And if one may descend to more trifling particulars, it is to this same lordship of the sea that the Athenians owe the discovery, in the first place, of many of the luxuries of life through intercourse with other countries. So that the choice things of Sicily and Italy, of Cyprus and Egypt and Lydia, of Pontus or Peloponnese, or wheresoever else it be, are all swept, as it were, into one center, and all owing, as I say, to their maritime empire. And again, in process of listening to every form of speech, they have selected this from one place and that from another — for themselves. So much so that while the rest of the Hellenes employ each pretty much their own peculiar mode of speech, habit of life, and style of dress, the Athenians have adopted a composite type, to which all sections of Hellas, and the foreigner alike, have contributed.

As regards sacrifices and temples and festivals and sanctuaries, the people sees that it is not possible for every poor citizen to do sacrifice and hold festival, or to set up temples and to inhabit a large and beautiful city. But it has hit upon a means of meeting the difficulty. They sacrifice — that is, the whole state sacrifices — at the public cost a large number of victims; but it is the people that keeps holiday and distributes the victims by lot among its members. Rich men have in some cases private gymnasia and baths with dressing rooms, but the people takes care to have built at the public cost a number of palaestras, dressing rooms, and bathing establishments for its own special use, and the mob gets the benefit of the majority of these, rather than the select few or the well-to-do.

As to wealth, the Athenians alone of Hellenes and foreigners are able to possess it. For if some state is rich in timber for shipbuilding, where is it to find a market for the product except by persuading the ruler of the sea? Or, suppose the wealth of some state or other consists of iron, or of bronze, or of linen yarn, where will it find a market except by permission of the supreme maritime power? Yet these are the very things, you see, which I need for my ships. Timber I must have from one, and from another iron, from a third bronze, from a fourth linen, from a fifth wax. Besides which they will not allow these to be carried elsewhere, or our competitors will not be allowed the use of the sea. Accordingly I without labor extract from the land and possess all these goods, thanks to my supremacy on the sea, while no single other state possesses any two of them. Timber and linen are not found in the same city, but where linen is abundant the soil will be light and devoid of timber. And in the same way bronze and iron will not be products of the same city. And so for the rest, never two, or at best three, in one state, but one thing here and another thing there.

Moreover, above and beyond what has been said, the coast line of every mainland presents either some jutting promontory or adjacent island or narrow strait of some sort, so that those who are masters of the sea can come to moorings at one of these points and wreak vengeance on the inhabitants of the mainland. There is just one thing which the Athenians lack. Supposing they were the inhabitants of an island and were still, as now, rulers of the sea, they would have had it in their power to work whatever mischief they liked and to suffer no evil in return (as long as they kept command of the sea), neither the ravaging of their territory nor the expectation of an enemy's approach. But at present the farming portion of the community and the wealthy landowners are ready to cringe before the enemy overmuch, while the people —

knowing full well that come what may not one stock or stone of their property will suffer, nothing will be cut down, nothing burnt — lives in freedom from alarm, without dreading the enemy. Besides this, there is another fear from which they would have been exempt in an island home — the apprehension of the city being at any time betrayed by their oligarchs and the gates thrown open, and an enemy bursting suddenly in. How could incidents like these have taken place if an island had been their home? Again, had they inhabited an island there would have been no stirring of sedition against the people; whereas at present, in the event of faction, those who set it on foot base their hopes of success on the introduction of an enemy by land. But a people inhabiting an island would be free from all anxiety on that score. Since, however, they did not chance to inhabit an island from the first, what they now do is this — they deposit their property in the islands, trusting to their command of the sea, and they suffer the soil of Attika to be ravaged without a sigh. To expend pity on that, they know, would be to deprive themselves of other blessings still more precious.

Further, states oligarchically governed are forced to ratify their alliances and solemn oaths, and if they fail to abide by their contracts the offense, by whomsoever committed, lies nominally at the door of the oligarchs who entered upon the contract. But in the case of engagements entered into by a democracy it is open to the people to throw the blame on the single individual who spoke in favor of some measure or put it to the vote, and to maintain to the rest of the world that it was not present nor does it approve unless the covenants are scrutinized in a full meeting of the people; and if these should not seem good, it has discovered ten thousand pretexts for not doing whatever it does not wish. And if any mischief should spring out of any resolutions which the people has passed in assembly, the people can readily shift the blame from its own shoulders: "A handful of oligarchs acting against the interests of the people have ruined us." But if any good result ensue, they, the people, at once take the credit of that to themselves.

In the same spirit it is not allowed to caricature on the comic stage or otherwise libel the people, because they do not care to hear themselves ill spoken of. But if any one has a desire to satirize his neighbor he has full leave to do so. And this because they are well aware that, as a general rule, the person caricatured does not belong to the people, or the masses. He is more likely to be some wealthy or well-born person, or man of means and influence. In fact, but few poor people and of the popular stamp incur the comic lash, or if they do they have brought it on themselves by excessive love of meddling or some covetous self-seeking at the expense of the people, so that no particular annoyance is felt at seeing such folk satirized.

What I venture to assert, then, is that the people of Athens has no difficulty in recognizing which of its citizens are of the better sort and which the opposite. And so recognizing those who are serviceable and advantageous to itself, even though they be base, the people loves them; but the good folk they are disposed the rather to hate. This virtue of theirs, the people holds, is not engrained in their nature for any good to itself, but rather for its injury. In direct opposition to this, there are some persons who, being born of the people, are yet by natural instinct not commoners. For my part I pardon the people its own democracy, as, indeed, it is pardonable in any one to do good to himself. But the man who, not being himself one of the people, prefers to live in a state democratically governed rather than in an oligarchical state may be said to smooth his own path towards iniquity. He knows that a bad man has a better chance of slipping through the fingers of justice in a democratic than in an oligarchical state.

I repeat that my position concerning the constitution of the Athenians is this: I do not approve of the type, but given that they have decided to have a democratic form of government, they do seem to me to go the right way to preserve the democracy by the adoption of the particular type which I have set forth.

But I am aware that other objections are brought against the Athenians by certain people, and to this effect. It not seldom happens, they tell us, that a man is unable to transact a piece of business with the council or the people, even if he sits waiting a whole year. Now this does happen at Athens, and for no other reason save that, owing to the immense mass of affairs they are unable to give audience to all and send them off. And how in the world should they be able, considering in the first place that they, the Athenians, have more festivals to celebrate than any other state throughout the length and breadth of Hellas? During these festivals, of course, the transaction of any sort of affairs of state is still more out of the question. In the next place, only consider the number of cases they have to decide, what with private suits and public causes and scrutinies of accounts, etc. — more than the whole of the rest of mankind put together; while the council has multifarious points to advise upon concerning war, concerning ways and means, concerning the passing of laws, and concerning the matters constantly arising in the city and endless questions touching the allies, besides the receipt of the tribute, the super-intendence of dockyards and temples, etc. Can, I ask again, any one find it at all surprising that, with all these affairs on their hands, they are unequal to doing business with all the world?

But some people tell us that if the applicant will only address himself to the council or the people with a fee in his hand he will do a good stroke of business. And for my part I am free to confess to these gainsayers that a good many things may be done at Athens by dint of money; and I will add, that a good many more still might be done, if the money flowed still more freely and from more pockets. One thing, however, I know full well, that as to transacting with every one of these applicants all he wants, the state could not do it, not even if all the gold and silver in the world were the inducement offered.

Here are some of the cases which have to be decided on. Some one fails to fit out a ship: judgment must be given. Another puts up a building on a piece of public land: again judgment must be given. Or, to take another class of cases: adjudication has to be made among potential candidates to provide choruses for the Dionysia, the Thargelia, the Panathenaia, year after year. And again, in behalf of the gymnasiarchs a similar adjudication for the Panathenaia, the Prometheia, and the Hephaistia, also year after year. Also as between the trierarchs, four hundred of whom are appointed each year, of these, too, any who choose must have their cases adjudicated on, year after year. But that is not all. There are various magistrates to examine and approve and decide between; there are orphans whose status must be examined, and guardians of prisoners to appoint. These, be it borne in mind, are all matters of yearly occurrence; while at intervals there are exemptions from military service which call for adjudication, or if some sudden offense occurs, some case of outrage and violence of an exceptional character, or some charge of impiety. A whole string of others I simply omit; I am content to have named the most important part — except for the assessments of tribute which occur, as a rule, at intervals of five years.

I put it to you, then: can any one suppose that all, or any, of these may dispense with adjudication? If so, will any one say which ought, and which ought not, to be adjudicated, there and then? If, on the other hand, we are forced to admit that these are all fair cases for adjudication, it follows of necessity that they should be decided during the twelve-month; since even now the boards of judges sitting right through the year are powerless to stay the tide of evildoing by reason of the multitude of the people.

So far so good. "But," some one will say, "try the cases you certainly must, but lessen the number of the judges." But if so, it follows of necessity that unless the courts themselves are diminished in number there will only be a few judges sitting in each court, with the further consequence that it will be easier to deal with few judges and bribe the whole body, to the greater detriment of justice.

But besides this we cannot escape the situation that the Athenians have their festivals to keep, during which the courts cannot sit. As a matter of fact these festivals are twice as numerous as those of any other people. But I will reckon them as merely equal to those of the state which has the fewest.

All this being so, I maintain that it is not possible for business affairs at Athens to stand on any very different footing from the present, except to some slight extent, by adding here and deducting there. Any large modification is out of the question, short of damaging the democracy itself. No doubt many expedients might be discovered for improving the constitution, but if the problem be to discover some adequate means of improving the constitution while at the same time the democracy is to remain intact, I say it is not easy to do this, except, as I have just stated, to the extent of some trifling addition here or deduction there.

There is another point in which it is sometimes felt that the Athenians are ill advised, in their adoption, namely, of the less respectable party, in a state divided by faction. But if so, they do it advisedly. If they chose the more respectable, they would be adopting those whose views and interests differ from their own, for there is no state in which the best element is friendly to the people. It is the worst element which in every state favors the democracy — on the principle that like favors like. It is simple enough then. The Athenians choose what is most akin to themselves. Also, on every occasion on which they have attempted to side with the better classes it has not fared well with them, but within a short interval the democratic party has been enslaved, as for instance in Boiotia; or, as when they chose the aristocrats of the Milesians, and within a short time these revolted and cut the people to pieces; or, as when they chose the Spartans as against the Messenians, and with a short time the Spartans subjugated the Messenians and went to war against Athens.

I seem to overhear a retort, "No one, of course, is deprived of his civil rights at Athens unjustly." My answer is, that there are some who are unjustly deprived of their civil rights, though the cases are certainly rare. But it will take more than a few to attack the democracy at Athens, since you may take it as an established fact, it is not the man who has lost his civil rights justly that takes the matter to heart, but the victims, if any, of injustice. But how in the world can any one imagine that many are in a state of civil disability at Athens, where the people and the holders of office are one and the same? It is from iniquitous exercise of office, from iniquity exhibited either in speech or action, and the like circumstances, that citizens are punished with deprivation of civil rights in Athens. Due reflection on these matters will serve to dispel the notion that there is any danger at Athens from persons visited with disfranchisement.

II...AND ELSEWHERE

RELIGIOUS TOLERANCE IN THE PERSIAN EMPIRE
Meiggs-Lewis 12

Found near Magnesia on the Meander River, this inscription contains the Greek version of a letter sent ca. 490 B.C. by the Persian king Darius to (apparently) his satrap in Ionia. The subject was still of interest in the second century A.D., when this copy of the text was inscribed.

The king of kings, Darius son of Hystaspes, speaks to his slave Gadatas: I learn that you are not obeying my orders in every respect. Because you improve my land by transplanting trans-Euphratan crops to the lower parts of Asia, I commend your purpose, and for this great favor will be stored up for you in the king's house.[63] But because you obscure my disposition respecting the gods, I will give you — unless you change — a taste of my anger when wronged: for you exacted tribute from the gardeners of (a shrine of) Apollo and ordered them to till secular land, ignoring the attitude of my forefathers toward the god, who told[64] the Persians the whole truth . . .

[The rest is lost.]

TREATY BETWEEN ELIS AND HERAIA
Meiggs-Lewis 17

This treaty, one of the earliest extant, dates from ca. 500 B.C. The absence of an oath and divine sanctions is unusual: perhaps they were sufficiently implied under the prevailing presence of Zeus at Olympia (in Elis). The translation is that of Meiggs and Lewis.

This is the covenant between Elis and Heraia. There shall be an alliance for a hundred years, and this (year) shall be the first; and if anything is needed, either word or deed, they shall stand by each other in all matters and especially in war; and if they stand not by each other, those who do the wrong shall pay a talent of silver to Olympian Zeus to be used in his service. And if anyone injures this writing, whether private man or magistrate or community, he shall be liable to the sacred fine herein written.

SPARTA, AN ARRESTED SOCIETY
Xenophon, *Constitution of Sparta*

Though composed ca. 375 B.C., this treatise portrays the classical picture of Sparta, as it appeared to its fifth-century admirers as well. The institutions described herein were credited to the legendary lawgiver Lykourgos, but in actuality represent the modifications and accretions of several centuries.

I

I recall the astonishment with which I first noted the unique position of Sparta among the states of Hellas, the relatively sparse population, and at the same time the extraordinary power and prestige of the community. I was puzzled to account for the fact. It was only when I came to consider the peculiar institutions of the Spartans that my wonderment ceased. Or rather, it is transferred to the legislator who gave them those laws, obedience to which has been the secret of their prosperity. This legislator, Lykourgos, I must needs admire, and hold him to have been one of the wisest of mankind. Certainly he was no servile imitator of other states. It was by a stroke of invention rather, and on a pattern much in opposition to the commonly-accepted one, that he brought his fatherland to this pinnacle of prosperity.

Take, for example — and it is well to begin at the beginning — the whole topic of the begetting and rearing of children. Throughout the rest of the world the young girl, who will one day become a mother (and I speak of those who may be held to be well brought up), is nurtured on the plainest food attainable, with the scantiest addition of meat or other condiments; while as to wine they train them either to total abstinence or to take it highly diluted with water. And in imitation, as it were, of the handicraft type, since the majority of artificers are sedentary, we, the rest of the Hellenes, are content that our girls should sit quietly and work wools. This is all we demand of them. But how are we to expect that women nurtured in this fashion should produce a splendid offspring?

Lykourgos pursued a different path. Clothes were things, he held, the furnishing of which might well enough be left to female slaves. And, believing that the highest function of a free woman was the bearing of children, in the first place he insisted on the training of the body as incumbent no less on the female than on the male; and in pursuit of the same idea he instituted contests in running and feats of strength for women as for men. His belief was that where both parents were strong their progeny would be found to be more vigorous.

And so again after marriage. In view of the fact that immoderate intercourse is elsewhere permitted during the earlier period of matrimony, he adopted a principle directly opposite. He laid it down as an ordinance that a man should be ashamed to be seen visiting the chamber of his wife, whether going in or coming out. When they did meet under such restraint the mutual longing of these lovers could not but be increased, and the fruit which might spring from such intercourse would tend to be more robust than theirs whose affections are cloyed by satiety. By a further step in the same direction he refused to allow marriages to be contracted at any period of life according to the fancy of the parties concerned. Marriage, as he ordained it, must only take place in the prime of bodily vigor, this too being, as he believed, a condition conducive to the production of healthy offspring. Or, in the case of an old man wedded to a young wife, considering the jealous watch which such husbands are apt to keep over their wives, he introduced a directly opposite custom; that is to say, he made it incumbent on the aged husband to introduce some one whose qualities, physical and moral, he admired, to play the husband's part and to beget him children. Or again, in the case of a man who might not desire to live with a wife permanently, but yet might be anxious to have children of his own worthy the name, the lawgiver laid down a law in his behalf; such an one might select some woman, the wife of some man, well born herself and blest with fair offspring, and, the sanction and consent of her husband first obtained, raise up children for himself through her.

These and many other adaptations of a like sort the lawgiver sanctioned. As, for instance, at Sparta a wife will not object to bear the burden of a double establishment, or a husband to adopt sons as foster-brothers of his own children, with a full share in his family and position, but possessing no claim to his wealth and property.

So opposed to those of the rest of the world are the

principles which Lykourgos devised in reference to the production of children. Whether they enabled him to provide Sparta with a race of men superior to all in size and strength I leave to the judgment of whomsoever it may concern

II

After this exposition of the customs in connection with the birth of children, I wish now to explain the systems of education in fashion here and elsewhere. Throughout the rest of Hellas the custom on the part of those who claim to educate their sons in the best way is as follows. As soon as the children are of an age to understand what is said to them they are immediately placed under the charge of paidagogoi, who are also attendants, and are sent off to the school of some teacher to be taught grammar, music, and the concerns of the palestra. Besides this they are given shoes to wear which tend to make their feet tender, and their bodies are enervated by various changes of clothing. As for food, the only measure recognized is that which is fixed by appetite.

But when we turn to Lykourgos, instead of leaving it to each member of the state privately to appoint a slave to be his son's tutor, he set over the young Spartans a public guardian, the paidonomos (educator) as he is called, with complete authority over them. This guardian was selected from those who filled the highest magistracies. He had authority to hold musters of the boys, and as their overseer, in case of any misbehavior, to chastise severely. The legislator further provided the educator with a body of youths in the prime of life and bearing whips, to inflict punishment when necessary, with this happy result that in Sparta modesty and obedience ever go hand in hand, nor is there lack of either.

Instead of softening their feet with shoe or sandal, his rule was to make them hardy through going barefoot. This habit if practised would, as he believed, enable them to scale heights more easily and clamber down precipices with less danger. In fact, with his feet so trained the young Spartan would leap and spring and run faster unshod than another shod in the ordinary way.

Instead of making them effeminate with a variety of clothes, his rule was to habituate them to a single garment the whole year through, thinking that so they would be better prepared to withstand the variations of heat and cold.

Again, as regards food, he counseled such moderation as to avoid that heaviness which is engendered by repletion, and yet not to remain altogether unacquainted with the pains of penurious living. His belief was that by such training in boyhood they would be better able when occasion demanded to continue toiling on an empty stomach. They would be all the fitter, if the word of command were given, to remain for a long stretch without extra dieting. The craving for luxuries would be less, the readiness to take any victual set before them greater, and in general the regimen would be found more healthy; under it they would increase in stature since, as he maintained, a diet which gave suppleness to the limbs must be more beneficial than one which added thickness to the bodily parts by feeding.

On the other hand, in order to guard against a too great pinch of starvation, though he did not actually allow the boys to help themselves without further trouble to what more they needed, he did give them permission to steal this thing or that in the effort to alleviate their hunger. It was certainly not from any real difficulty of supplying them with nutriment that he left them to provide themselves by this crafty method, nor can I conceive that any one will so misinterpret the custom. Clearly its explanation lies in the fact that he who would live the life of a robber must forgo sleep by night, and in the daytime he must employ shifts and lie in ambuscade; he must prepare and make ready his scouts, and so forth, if he is to succeed in capturing the quarry.

It is obvious that the whole of this education tended, and was intended, to make the boys craftier and more inventive in getting supplies, while at the same time it cultivated their warlike instincts. An objector may retort: "But if he thought it so fine a feat to steal, why did he inflict all those blows on the unfortunate who was caught?" My answer is: for the selfsame reason which induces people, in other matters which are taught, to punish the malperformance of a service. So they, the Spartans, visit penalties on the boy who is detected thieving as being but a sorry bungler in the art. So to steal as many cheeses as possible was a feat to be encouraged; but, at the same moment, others were enjoined to scourge the thief, which would point a moral not obscurely, that by pain endured for a brief season a man may earn the joyous reward of lasting glory. Herein, too, it is plainly shown that where speed is requisite the sluggard will win for himself much trouble and scant good.

Furthermore, and in order that the boys should not want a guide even if the paidonomos himself were absent, he gave to any citizen who chanced to be present authority to lay upon them injunctions for their good, and to chastise them for any trespass committed. By so doing he created in the boys of Sparta a rare modesty. And indeed there is nothing which, whether as boys or men, they respect more highly than these guides. Lastly, and with the same intention, that the boys must never be without a guide, he laid down the rule that, if by chance there were no grown man present, the sharpest of the twenty-year-olds was to serve as guide of each group. Thus the boys of Sparta are never without a guide.

I ought not, I think, omit some remark on the subject of boy attachments, it being a topic in close connection with that of boyhood and the training of boys.

We know that the rest of the Hellenes deal with this relationship in different ways, either after the manner of the Boiotians, where man and boy are intimately united by a bond like that of wedlock, or after the manner of the Eleians, where the fruition of beauty is an act of grace; while there are others who would absolutely debar the lover from all conversation and discourse with the beloved.

Lykourgos adopted a system opposed to all of these alike. If some one, being himself all that a man ought to be, should in admiration of a boy's soul endeavour to discover in him a true friend without reproach and to consort with him — this was a relationship which Lykourgos commended and indeed regarded as the noblest type of bringing up. But if it was evidently not an attachment to the soul but a yearning merely towards the body, he stamped this thing as foul and horrible. The result is, to the credit of Lykourgos be it said, that in Sparta the relationship of lover and beloved is like that of parent and child or brother and brother, where carnal appetite is in abeyance. That this, however, which is the fact, should be scarcely credited in some quarters does not surprise me, seeing that in many states the laws do not oppose the desires in question.

I have now described the two chief methods of education in vogue; that is to say, the Spartan as contrasted with that of the rest of Hellas, and I leave it to him whom it may concern to judge which of the two has produced the finer type of men. And by finer I mean the better disciplined, the more modest and reverential, and, in matters where self-restraint is a virtue, the more continent.

III

When boys advance from boyhood to youth, just then the rest of the world emancipate their children from the private tutor and the schoolmaster, and, without substituting any further guide, launch them into absolute independence. Here, again, Lykourgos took an entirely opposite view of the matter. This, if observation may be trusted, was the season when the tide of animal spirits flows fast, and the froth of insolence rises to the surface; when, too, the most violent appetites for divers pleasures are aroused. This, then, was the right moment at which to impose tenfold labors upon the growing youth, and to devise for him a subtle system of absorbing occupation. And by a crowning enactment, which said that "he who shrank from the duties imposed on him would forfeit henceforth all claim to the glorious honors of the state," he caused not only the public authorities but those personally interested in the several companies of youths to take serious pains so that no one of them should by an act of craven cowardice find himself utterly rejected and reprobate within the body politic.

Furthermore, in his desire firmly to implant in their youthful souls a root of modesty he imposed upon these bigger boys a special rule: in the streets they were to keep their two hands within the folds of the cloak; they were to walk in silence and without turning their heads to gaze about, but rather to keep their eyes fixed upon the ground before them. And hereby it would seem to be proved conclusively that, even in the matter of quiet bearing and sobriety, the masculine type may claim greater strength than that which we attribute to the nature of women. At any rate, you might sooner expect a stone image to find voice than one of those Spartan youths; to divert the eyes of some bronze

statue were less difficult. And as to quiet bearing, no bride ever
stepped in bridal bower with more natural modesty. Note them
when they have reached the public table: the plainest answer to
the question asked — that is all you need expect to hear from their
lips.

IV

But if he was thus careful in the education of the stripling,
the Spartan lawgiver showed still greater anxiety in dealing with
those who had reached the prime of opening manhood, considering their immense importance to the city in the scale of good, if
only they proved themselves the men they should be. He had only
to look around to see that wherever the spirit of emulation is most
deeply seated, there too their choruses and gymnastic contests will
present alike a far higher charm to eye and ear. And on the same
principle he persuaded himself that he needed only to confront his
youthful warriors in the strife of valor, and with like result. They
also, in their degree, might be expected to attain to some
unknown height of manly virtue.

The method he adopted to engage these combatants I will
now explain. Their ephors select three men out of the whole body
of the citizens in the prime of life. These three men are named
hippagretai (masters of the horse). Each of these selects one
hundred others, explaining for what reason he prefers these and
rejects those. Thus those who fail to obtain the distinction are at
open war with those who rejected them and with those who were
chosen in their stead; and they keep ever a jealous eye on one
another for some misdeed contrary to the code of honor there
held customary. And so is set on foot that strife to the gods most
pleasing and for the purposes of state most politic. It is a strife in
which not only is the pattern of a brave man's conduct fully set
forth, but where, too, each against other and in separate camps the
rival parties train for victory. One day the superiority shall be
theirs; or, in the day of need, one and all to the last man they will
be ready to aid the fatherland with all their strength.

Necessity, moreover, is laid upon them to study a good habit
of the body, coming as they do to blows with their fists for strife's
sake wherever they meet. Still, any one present has a right to

separate the combatants, and if obedience is not shown to the peacemaker the paidonomos hales the delinquent before the ephors and the ephors inflict heavy damages, since they will have it plainly understood that rage must never override obedience to law.

With regard to those who have already passed the vigor of early manhood and on whom the highest magistracies henceforth devolve, there is a like contrast. In Hellas generally we find that at this age the need of further attention to physical strength is removed, although the imposition of military service continues. But Lykourgos made it customary for that section of his citizens to regard hunting as the highest honor suited to their age, albeit not to the exclusion of any public duty. And his aim was that they might be able to undergo the fatigues of war equally with those in the prime of manhood.

V

Having described the institutions legislated by Lykourgos for each age group, I shall now endeavor to relate the style of living which he established for the whole body. It will be understood that when Lykourgos first came to deal with the question the Spartans, like the rest of the Hellenes, used to dine at home. Tracing most misdeeds to this custom, he brought common meals into broad daylight, expecting thus to minimize the transgression of orders.

As to food, his ordinance allowed them so much as, while not inducing repletion, should guard them from actual want. And, in fact, there are many exceptional dishes in the form of game supplied from the hunting field. Or, as a substitute for these, rich men will occasionally garnish the feast with wheaten loaves. So that from beginning to end, till they separate, the common board is never stinted for viands nor yet extravagant.

So also in the matter of drink, while putting a stop to all unnecessary potations, detrimental alike to a firm brain and a steady gait, he left them free to quench thirst when nature dictated — a method which would add to the pleasure while it diminished the danger of drinking. And indeed one may fairly ask how, in such a system of common meals, it would be possible for any one to ruin either himself or his family through either gluttony or winebibbing.

This too must be borne in mind, that in other states equals in age for the most part associate together, and such an atmosphere is little conducive to modesty. But in Sparta Lykourgos mixed the age groups together, so that the younger men benefit largely from the experience of the older, since it is their custom in the dining halls to talk about honorable acts performed in the state. The scene, in fact, lends itself but little to the intrusion of violence or drunken riot; ugly speech and ugly deeds alike are out of place. Among other good results obtained through this outdoor system of meals may be mentioned this: There is the necessity of walking home when the meal is over and a consequent anxiety not to be caught tripping under the influence of wine, since they all know of course that the supper table must be presently abandoned and they must move as freely in the dark as in the day, even the help of a torch to guide the steps being forbidden to all on active service.

In connection with this matter, Lykourgos had not failed to observe the effect of equal amounts of food on different persons. The hardworking man has a good complexion, he is robust and strong. The man who abstains from work, on the other hand, may be detected by his miserable appearance; he is blotched and puffy, and devoid of strength. This observation was not wasted on him. On the contrary, considering that any one who chooses as a matter of private judgment to devote himself to toil may hope to present a very creditable appearance physically, he enjoined upon the eldest in every gymnasium to see to it that the labors of the class were proportional to the food. And to my mind he was not mistaken in this matter either. At any rate, it would be hard to discover a healthier or more completely developed human being, physically speaking, than the Spartan: their gymnastic training, in fact, makes demands alike on the legs and arms and neck.

VI

There are other points in which this legislator's views run counter to those commonly accepted. Thus, in other states the individual citizen is master over his own children, domestics, goods and chattels, and belongings generally; but Lykourgos, whose aim was to secure to all the citizens a considerable share in one another's goods without mutual injury, enacted that each one should have an equal power over his neighbor's children as over his own. The principle is this: when a man knows that this, that, and the other person are fathers of children subject to his own authority, he must perforce deal by them even as he desires his own children to be dealt by. And, if a boy chance to have received a whipping, not from his own father but some other, and goes and complains to his own father, it would be thought wrong on the part of that father if he did not inflict a second whipping on his son. A striking proof, in its way, of how completely they trust each other not to impose dishonorable commands upon their children.

In the same way he empowered them to use their neighbor's domestics in case of need. This community he applied also to hunting dogs: a party in need of dogs will invite the owner to the hunt, and if he is not at leisure to attend himself he is happy to let his dogs go. The same applies to the use of horses: someone has fallen sick perhaps, or is in want of a carriage, or is anxious to reach some point or other quickly — in any case he has a right, if he sees a horse anywhere, to take and use it, and he restores it safe and sound when he has done with it.

And here is another practice he instituted not customary elsewhere. A hunting party returns from the chase, belated. They want provisions — they have nothing prepared themselves. To meet this contingency he made it a rule that owners are to leave food prepared in lockers: the party in need will open the seals, take out what they want, seal up the the remainder, and leave it. Accordingly, by his system of give-and-take even those with next to nothing have a share in all that the country can supply, if ever they stand in need of anything.

VII

There are yet other customs in Sparta which Lykourgos instituted in opposition to those of the rest of Hellas, among them the following. We all know that in the other states every one makes as much money as he can — one man as a tiller of the soil, another as a mariner, a third as a merchant, while others depend on various arts to earn a living. But at Sparta Lykourgos forbade his freeborn citizens to have anything whatsoever to do with the concerns of money-making. As freemen, he enjoined upon them to regard as their concern exclusively those activities upon which the foundations of civic liberty are based.

And indeed, one may well ask, why should wealth be regarded as a matter for serious pursuit in a community where, partly by a system of equal contributions to the necessaries of life and partly by the maintenance of a common standard of living, the lawgiver placed so effectual a check upon the desire for riches for the sake of luxury? What inducement, for instance, would there be to make money, even for the sake of wearing apparel, in a state where personal adornment is held to lie not in the costliness of the clothes worn, but in the healthy condition of the body to be clothed? Nor again could there be much inducement to amass wealth in order to be able to expend it on participants in common meals, since the legislator had made it seem far more glorious that a man should help his fellows by the labor of his body than by costly outlay — the latter being, as he finely phrased it, the function of wealth, the former an activity of the soul.

He went a step further and set up a strong barrier (even in a society such as I have described) against the pursuance of money-making by wrongful means. In the first place, he established a coinage of so extraordinary a sort that even a sum of ten minas could not come into a house without attracting the notice of the master himself or of some member of his household: in fact, it would occupy a considerable space, and need a wagon to carry it. Gold and silver, moreover, are liable to search, and if any is found anywhere the possessor is fined. In fact, to repeat the question asked above, for what reason should money-making become an earnest pursuit in a community where the possession of wealth entails more pain than its employment brings satisfaction?

VIII

But to proceed. We are all aware that there is no state in the world in which greater obedience is shown to magistrates, and to the laws themselves, than Sparta. But, for my part, I am disposed to think that Lykourgos could never have attempted to establish this healthy condition until he had first secured the unanimity of the most powerful members of the state. I infer this for the following reasons. In other states the leaders in rank and influence do not desire even to be thought to fear the magistrates. Such a thing they would regard as in itself a symbol of servility. In Sparta, on the contrary, the stronger a man is the more readily does he bow before constituted authority. And indeed, they pride themselves on their humility and on a prompt obedience, running, or at any rate not crawling with laggard step, at the word of command. They are convinced that such an example of eager discipline, set by themselves, will not fail to be followed by the rest. And this is precisely what has taken place. It is reasonable to suppose that these same ones helped establish the power of the ephorate, after they had come to the conclusion themselves that of all the blessings which a state or an army or a household can enjoy, obedience is the greatest — since, as they could not but reason, the greater the power with which men fence about authority, the greater the fascination it will exercise upon the mind of the citizen to the enforcement of obedience.

Accordingly the ephors are competent to punish whomsoever they choose; they have power to exact fines on the spur of the moment; they have power to depose magistrates in mid-career — nay, actually to imprison and bring them to trial on the capital charge. Entrusted with these vast powers, they do not, as do the rest of states, allow the elected magistrates to exercise authority as they like, right through the year of office; but, in the style rather of despotic monarchs or presidents of gymnastic games, at the first sign of any transgression they inflict chastisement without warning and without hesitation.

But of all the many beautiful contrivances invented by Lykourgos to kindle a willing obedience to the laws in the hearts of the citizens, none, to my mind, was happier or more excellent than his unwillingness to deliver his code to the people at large, until, attended by the most powerful members of the state, he had betaken himself to Delphi and there made inquiry of the god whether it were better for Sparta and conducive to her interests to obey the laws which he had framed. And not until the divine answer came: "Better will it be in every way," did he deliver them, laying it down that to refuse obedience to sanctions of the Pythian god was not only unlawful but also unholy.

IX

The following too may well excite our admiration for Lykourgos. I speak of the consummate skill with which he induced the whole state of Sparta to regard an honorable death as preferable to an ignoble life. And indeed if any one will investigate the matter, he will find that by comparison with those who make it a principle to retreat in face of danger actually fewer of these Spartans die in battle, since, to speak truth, it seems that salvation attends on virtue far more frequently than on cowardice — virtue, which is at once easier and sweeter, richer in resource and stronger of arm, than her opposite. And that virtue has another familiar attendant — to wit, glory — needs no showing, since all want to fight with the good in some fashion.

Yet the actual means by which he gave currency to these principles is a point which it were well not to overlook. It is clear that the lawgiver set himself deliberately to provide all the blessings of heaven for the good man, and a sorry and ill-starred existence for the coward.

In other states the man who shows himself base and cowardly wins to himself an evil reputation and the nickname of a coward, but that is all. For the rest he buys and sells in the same marketplace with the good man; he sits beside him at the play; he exercises with him in the same gymnasium, and all as suits his humor. But at Sparta there is not one man who would not feel ashamed to accept the coward as a messmate or as a partner in a wrestling bout. Consider the day's round of his existence. The sides are being chosen in a ball game, but he is left out as the odd man; there is no place for him. During the choric dance he is driven away into ignominious places. Nay, in the very streets it is he who must step aside for others to pass, or, being seated, he must rise and make room, even for a younger man. At home he will have his maiden relatives to support in their isolation (and they will hold him to blame for their unwedded lives). A hearth with no wife to bless it — that is a condition he must face, and at the same time he will have to pay a penalty for it. Let him not roam abroad with a smooth and smiling countenance; let him not imitate men whose fame is irreproachable, or he shall feel on his back the blows of his superiors. Such being the weight of infamy which is laid upon all cowards, I, for my part, am not surprised if in Sparta they deem death preferable to a life so steeped in dishonor and reproach.

X

That too was a happy enactment, in my opinion, by which Lykourgos provided for the continual cultivation of virtue, even to old age. By fixing election to the council of elders at the end of life, he made it impossible for a high standard of virtuous living to be disregarded even in old age. So, too, it is worthy of admiration in him that he lent his helping hand to virtuous old age. Thus, by making the elders sole arbiters in the trial for life, he contrived to charge old age with a greater weight of honor than that which is accorded to the strength of mature manhood. And assuredly such a contest as this must appeal to the zeal of mortal man beyond all others in supreme degree. Fair, doubtless, are contests of gymnastic skill, yet they are but trials of bodily excellence, but this contest for the council of elders is an ordeal of the soul itself. In proportion, therefore, as the soul is worthier than the body, so must these contests of the soul be worthier of zealous endeavor than those of the body.

And yet another point may well excite great admiration for Lykourgos. It had not escaped his observation that communities exist where those who are willing to make virtue their study and delight fail somehow in ability to add to the glory of their fatherland. That lesson the legislator laid to heart, and in Sparta he enforced, as a matter of public duty, the practice of every virtue by every citizen. And so, just as man differs from man in some excellence according as he cultivates or neglects to cultivate it, this city of Sparta, with good reason, outshines all other states in virtue; since she, and she alone, has made the attainment of a high standard of noble living a public duty.

And was not this a noble enactment, that whereas other states are content to inflict punishment only in cases where a man does wrong against his neighbor, Lykourgos imposed penalties no less severe on him who openly neglected to make himself as good as possible? For this, it seems, was his principle: in the one case, where a man is robbed, or defrauded, or kidnapped and made a slave, the injury of the misdeed is personal to the individual so maltreated; but in the other case whole communities suffer foul treason at the hand of the base man and the coward. So that it was only reasonable, in my opinion, that he should visit the heaviest penalty upon these latter.

Moreover he laid upon them, like some irresistible necessity, the obligation to cultivate the whole virtue of a citizen. Provided they duly performed the injunctions of the law, the city belonged to them, each and all, in absolute possession and on an equal footing. Weakness of limb or want of wealth was no drawback in his eyes. But as for him who shrank from the painful performance of the law's injunction out of cowardice, the finger of the legislator pointed him out as there and then disqualified to be regarded longer as a member of the brotherhood of peers.

It may be added, that there is no doubt as to the great antiquity of this code of laws. The point is clear so far, that Lykourgos himself is said to have lived in the days of the Herakleidai. But being of so long standing, these laws, even at this day, still are stamped in the eyes of other men with all the novelty of youth. And the most marvelous thing of all is that, while everybody is agreed to praise these remarkable institutions, there is not a single state which cares to imitate them.

XI

The above form a common stock of blessings, open to every Spartan to enjoy, alike in peace and in war. But if any one desires to be informed in what way the legislator improved upon the ordinary machinery of warfare and in reference to an army in the field, it is easy to satisfy his curiosity.

In the first instance, the ephors announce by proclamation the limit of age to which the service applies for cavalry and heavy infantry; and in the next place, for the various handicraftsmen. So that, even on active service, the Spartans are well supplied with all the conveniences enjoyed by people living as citizens at home. All implements and instruments whatsoever, which an army may need in common, are ordered to be in readiness, some on wagons and others on baggage animals. In this way anything omitted can hardly escape detection.

For the actual encounter under arms, the following inventions are attributed to Lykourgos. The soldier has a crimson uniform and a heavy shield of bronze, his theory being that such an equipment has no sort of feminine associations and is altogether most warrior-like. It is most quickly burnished; it is least readily soiled.

He further permitted those who were above the age of early manhood to wear their hair long. For so, he conceived, they would appear of larger stature, more free and indomitable, and of a more terrible aspect.

He divided his citizen soldiers, so furnished and accoutred, into six *morai* (divisions) of cavalry and heavy infantry. Each of the infantry *morai* has one polemarch, four lochagoi, eight penteconters and sixteen enomotarchs. At the word of command these *morai* can be formed now into *enomotiai,* now into three, or into six.

As to the commonly entertained idea that the tactical arrangement of the Lakonian heavy infantry is highly complicated, no conception could be more opposed to fact. For in the Lakonian order the front-rank men are all leaders, so that each file has everything necessary to play its part efficiently. In fact, this disposition is so easy to understand that no one who can distinguish one human being from another could fail to follow it. One set have the assignment of leading, the other the duty of following. The deployments by which greater depth or shallowness is given to the battle line, are announced by the enomotarch, who plays the part of herald, and they cannot be mistaken. None of these manoeuvres presents any difficulty whatsoever to the understanding.

As for fighting even if they are thrown into confusion by some mischance, I admit that the tactics here are not so easy to understand, except for people trained under the laws of Lykourgos. Even movements which an instructor in heavy-armed warfare might look upon as difficult are performed by the Spartans with the utmost ease. Thus, suppose the troops are marching in column; one section of a company is of course stepping up behind another from the rear. Now, if at such a moment a hostile force appears in front in battle order, the word is passed down to the commander of each section, "Deploy (into line) to the left." And so throughout the whole length of the column, until the line is formed facing the enemy. Or supposing while in this position an enemy appears in the rear. Each file performs a countermarch with the effect of bringing the best men face to face with the enemy all along the line. As to the point that the leader previously on the right finds himself now on the left, they do not consider that they are necessarily losers thereby but, as it may turn out, even gainers. If, for instance, the enemy attempted to turn their flank, he would find himself wrapping round, not their exposed, but their shielded flank. Or if, for any reason, it be thought advisable for the general to have the right wing, they turn the corps about and countermarch by ranks until the general is on the right and the rear rank on the left. Or again, supposing a division of the enemy appears on the right while they are marching in column, they have nothing further to do but to wheel each company to the right, like a trireme, prow forwards, to meet the enemy, and thus the rear company again finds itself on the right. If, however, the enemy should attack on the left, either they will not allow that and push him aside, or else they wheel their companies to the left to face the antagonist and thus the rear company once more falls into position on the left.

XII

I will now speak of the mode of encampment sanctioned by the regulation of Lykourgos. To avoid the waste incidental to the angles of a square the encampment, according to him, should be circular, except where there was the security of a hill or fortification, or where they had a river in their rear. He had sentinels posted during the day along the place of arms and facing inwards; since they are appointed not so much for the sake of the enemy as to keep an eye on friends. The enemy is sufficiently watched by mounted troopers perched on various points commanding the widest prospect.

To guard against hostile approach by night, sentinel duty according to the ordinance was performed by the skiritai (light armed) outside the main body. At the present time the rule is so far modified that the duty is entrusted to foreigners, if there be any, with a few Spartans to keep them company. The custom of always taking their spears with them when they go their rounds must certainly be attributed to the same cause which makes them exclude their slaves from the place of arms; nor need we be surprised if, when retiring for necessary purposes, they withdraw only far enough from one another or from their arms not to annoy one another — all done for safety's sake.

The frequency with which they change their encampments is another point. It is done quite as much for the sake of benefiting their friends as of harming their enemies.

Further, the law enjoins upon all Spartans during the whole period of an expedition the constant practice of gymnastic exercises, whereby their pride in themselves is increased and they appear freer than the rest of the world. The walking and running ground must not exceed in length the space covered by a *mora*, so that no one may find himself far from his own stand of arms. After the gymnastic exercises the senior polemarch gives the order (by herald) to be seated. This serves all the purposes of an inspection. After this the order is given to get breakfast, and for the outposts to be relieved. After this, again, come pastimes and relaxations before the evening exercises, after which the herald's cry is heard to take the evening meal. When they have sung a hymn to the gods to whom the offerings of happy omen have been performed, the final order, to retire to rest at the place of arms, is given.

The reader must not be surprised that I write at length, since it would be difficult to find any point demanding attention in military matters that has been neglected by the Spartans.

XIII

I will now give a detailed account of the power and privilege assigned by Lykourgos to the king during a military campaign. To begin with, so long as he is on active service the state maintains the king and those with him. The polemarchs eat with him and share his quarters, so that by dint of constant intercourse they may be all the better able to take common counsel in case of need. Three other members of the peers also share the royal quarters. The duty of these is to attend to all matters of commissariat, in order that the king and the rest may have unbroken leisure to attend to affairs of actual warfare.

But I will resume and describe the manner in which the king sets out with an army. As a preliminary step, before leaving home he offers sacrifice (in company with his staff) to Zeus Agetor (the Leader), and if the victims prove favorable then and there the priest takes some of the sacred fire off the altar and leads the way to the boundaries of the land. Here for the second time the king does sacrifice to Zeus and Athena; and as soon as the offerings are accepted by those two divinities he steps across the boundaries of the land. All the while the fire from those sacrifices leads the way and is never allowed to go out. Behind follow sacrificial beasts of every sort.

Invariably when he offers sacrifice the king begins the work in the gloaming before the day has broken, being minded to anticipate the goodwill of the god. And round about the place of sacrifice are present the polemarchs, lochagoi, penteconters, enomotarchs, leaders of the baggage train, and from other states any general who may care to assist. There, too, are to be seen two of the ephors, who meddle in nothing save only at the summons of the king, yet have their eyes fixed on the proceedings of each one there and keep all in order, as may be expected. When the sacrifices are accomplished the king summons all and issues his orders as to what has to be done. And all with such method that, to witness the proceedings, you might fairly suppose the rest of the world to be but bungling experimenters and the Spartans alone true handicraftsmen in the art of soldiering.

Anon the king puts himself at the head of the troops, and if no enemy appears he heads the line of march, no one preceding him except the skiritai and the mounted troopers exploring in front. If, however, there is any reason to anticipate a battle, the king takes the leading column of the first *mora* and wheels to the right until he is in the middle with two *morai* and two polemarchs on either flank. The disposition of the supports is assigned to the eldest of the royal council — the supports consisting of all peers who share the royal quarters, with the soothsayers, surgeons, pipers, leaders of the troops, and any volunteers who happen to be present. Thus, there is no difficulty about anything needing to be done; nothing is overlooked.

The following details also seem to me of high utility among the inventions of Lykourgos with a view to the final arbitrament of battle. When the enemy is close enough to watch the proceedings, the goat is sacrificed and all the pipers in their places play upon the pipes and every Spartan dons a wreath. Then too, so runs the order, let the shields be brightly polished. The privilege is afforded to the young man to enter battle with his long locks combed. To be of a cheery countenance — that, too, is of good repute. They pass the word of command on to the enomotarch, since it is impossible to hear along the whole of each section from each enomotarch posted on the outside. It devolves, finally, on the polemarch to see that all goes well.

When the right moment for encamping has come, the king is responsible for that, and has to point out the proper place. The despatch of embassies, however, whether to friends or to foes, is not the king's affair. Petitioners in general wishing to transact anything treat, in the first instance, with the king. If someone comes wanting justice, the king despatches him to the Hellano-dikai, if money, to the paymasters; if the petitioner brings booty, he is sent off to the laphuropolai (sellers of spoil). This being the mode of procedure, no other duty is left to the king, while he is on active service, except to play the part of priest in matters concerning the gods and of commander-in-chief in his relationship to men.

XIV

Now, if the question be put to me, Do you maintain that the laws of Lykourgos remain still to this day unchanged? that indeed is an assertion which I should no longer venture to maintain; knowing, as I do, that in former times the Spartans preferred to live at home on moderate means, content to associate exclusively with themselves rather than to play the part of governor-general in foreign states and to be corrupted by flattery; knowing further, as I do, that formerly they dreaded to be detected in the possession of gold, whereas nowadays there are not a few who make it their glory and their boast to be possessed of it. I am very well aware that in former days aliens were expelled for this very reason, and to live abroad was not allowed. And why? Simply in order that the citizens of Sparta might not take the infection of self-indulgence from foreigners; whereas now I am very well aware that those who are reputed to be leading citizens have but one ambition, and that is to live to the end of their days as governors-general on a foreign soil. The days were when their sole anxiety was to fit themselves to lead the rest of Hellas. But nowadays they concern themselves much more to wield command than to fit themselves to rule. And so it has come to pass that whereas in the past the Greeks came to Sparta seeking her leadership against reputed wrongdoers, now many are calling on one another to prevent the Spartans from ruling over them again. Yet we need not wonder if they have incurred all these reproaches, seeing that they are so plainly disobedient to the god himself and to the laws of their own lawgiver Lykourgos.

XV

I wish to explain with sufficient detail the nature of the covenant between king and state as instituted by Lykourgos; for this, I take it, is the sole type of rule which still preserves the original form in which it was first established; whereas other constitutions will be found either to have been already modified or else to be still undergoing modifications at this moment.

He laid it down as law that the king shall offer in behalf of the state all public sacrifices, as being himself of divine descent, and shall lead wherever the state despatches an army. He granted him to receive honorary gifts from the sacrifices, and he assigned him choice land in may of the subject cities, enough to satisfy moderate needs without excess of wealth. And in order that the kings also might dine in public he assigned them a public banquet, and he honored them with a double portion each at the evening meal, not in order that they might actually eat twice as much as others, but that the king might have wherewithal to honor whomsoever he desired. He also granted each of the kings to choose two messmates called pythioi. He also granted them to receive out of every litter of swine one pig, so that the king might never be at a loss for sacrificial victims if in aught he wished to consult the gods.

Close by the palace a lake affords an unrestricted supply of water; and how useful that is for various purposes they best can tell who lack that luxury. All rise from their seats for the king, but ephors do not rise from their seats of office. Monthly they exchange oaths, the ephors in behalf of the state, the king himself in his own behalf. This is the oath on the king's part: "I will exercise my kingship in accordance with the established laws of the state." And on the part of the state the oath runs: "So long as he (who exercises kingship) shall abide by his oath we will not suffer his kingdom to be shaken."

These then are the honors bestowed upon the king at home during his lifetime — honors by no means much exceeding those of private citizens, since the lawgiver was minded neither to instill in the kings the pride of the despotic monarch nor to engender in the citizens envy of their power. As to those other honors which are given to the king at his death, the laws of Lykourgos would seem plainly to signify hereby that these kings of Sparta are not mere mortals but heroic beings, and that is why they are preferred in honor.

THE EARTHQUAKE AT SPARTA
AND THE HELOT REVOLT, 464 B.C.
Diodoros of Sicily 11.63-64

During this year a great and incredible catastrophe befell the Lakedaimonians; for great earthquakes occurred in Sparta, and as a result the houses collapsed from their foundations and more than twenty thousand Lakedaimonians perished. And since the tumbling down of the city and the falling in of the houses continued uninterruptedly over a long period, many persons were caught and crushed in the collapse of the walls and no little household property was ruined by the quake. And although they suffered this disaster because some god, as it were, was wreaking his anger upon them, it so happened that other dangers befell them at the hands of men for the following reasons. The Helots and Messenians, although enemies of the Lakedaimonians, had remained quiet up to this time, since they stood in fear of the eminent position and power of Sparta; but when they observed that the larger part of them had perished because of the earthquake, they held in contempt the survivors, who were few. Consequently they came to an agreement with each other and joined together in the war against the Lakedaimonians. The king of the Lakedaimonians, Archidamos, by his personal foresight not only was the savior of his fellow citizens even during the earthquake, but in the course of the war also he bravely fought the aggressors. For instance, when the terrible earthquake struck Sparta, he was the first Spartan to seize his armor and hasten from the city into the country, calling upon the other citizens to follow his example. The Spartans obeyed him and thus those who survived the shock were saved, and these men King Archidamos organized into an army and prepared to make war upon the revolters.

The Messenians together with the Helots at first advanced against the city of Sparta, assuming that they would take it because there would be no one to defend it; but when they heard that the survivors were drawn up in a body with Archidamos the king and were ready for the struggle on behalf of their native land, they gave up this plan, and seizing a stronghold in Messenia they made it their base of operations and from there continued to overrun Lakonia. And the Spartans, turning for help to the Athenians, received from them an army; and they gathered troops as well from the rest of their allies and thus became able to meet their enemy on equal terms. At the outset they were much superior to the enemy, but at a later time, when a suspicion arose that the Athenians were about to go over to the Messenians, they broke the alliance with them, stating as their reason that in the other allies they had sufficient men to meet the impending battle. The Athenians, although they believed that they had suffered an affront, at the time did no more than withdraw; later, however, their relations to the Lakedaimonians being unfriendly, they were more and more inclined to fan the flames of hatred. Consequently the Athenians took this incident as the first cause of the estrangement of the two states, and later on they quarrelled and, embarking upon great wars, filled all Greece with vast calamities. But we shall give an account of these matters severally in connection with the appropriate periods of time. At the time in question the Lakedaimonians together with their allies marched forth against Ithome and laid siege to it. And the Helots, revolting in a body from the Lakedaimonians, joined as allies with the Messenians, and at one time they were winning and at another losing. And since for ten years no decision could be reached in the war, for that length of time they never ceased injuring each other.

SYRACUSE DEFEATS THE ETRUSCANS
Meiggs-Lewis 29

An early record from the western Greek world is this Greek inscription on an Etruscan helmet dedicated at Olympia by Hieron, tyrant of Syracuse, after his naval victory at Kyme (474 B.C.). A second such helmet, similarly inscribed, was found in 1959.

Hieron son of Deinomeneus and the Syracusans (dedicated) to Zeus the Etruscan spoils from Kyme.

END OF THE TYRANNY AT SYRACUSE, 466 B.C.
Diodoros of Sicily 11.67-68

During this year Thrasyboulos, the king of the Syracusans, was driven from his throne, and since we are writing a detailed account of this event, we must go back a few years and set forth clearly the whole story from the beginning.

Gelon, the son of Deinomeneus, who far excelled all other men in valor and strategy and out-generalled the Carthaginians, defeated these barbarians in a great battle; and since he treated the peoples whom he had subdued with fairness and, in general, conducted himself humanely toward all his immediate neighbors, he enjoyed high favor among the Sicilian Greeks. Thus Gelon, being beloved by all because of his mild rule, lived in uninterrupted peace until his death. But Hieron, the next oldest among the brothers, who succeeded to the throne, did not rule over his subjects in the same manner; for he was avaricious and violent and, speaking generally, an utter stranger to sincerity and nobility of character. Consequently there were a good many who wished to revolt, but they restrained their inclinations because of Gelon's reputation and the goodwill he had shown towards all the Sicilian Greeks. After the death of Hieron, however, his brother Thrasyboulos, who succeeded to the throne, surpassed in wickedness his predecessor in the kingship. For being a violent man and murderous by nature, he put to death many citizens unjustly and drove not a few into exile on false charges, confiscating their possessions into the royal treasury; and since, speaking generally, he hated those he had wronged and was hated by them, he enlisted a large body of mercenaries, preparing in this way a legion with which to oppose the citizen soldiery. And since he kept incurring more and more the hatred of the citizens by outraging many and executing others, he compelled the victims to revolt. Consequently the Syracusans, choosing men who would take the lead, set about as one man to destroy the tyranny, and once they had been organized by their leaders they clung stubbornly to their freedom. When Thrasyboulos saw that the whole city was in arms against him, he at first attempted to stop the revolt by persuasion; but after he observed that the movement of the Syracusans could not be halted, he gathered together both the colonists whom Hieron had settled in Katana and his other allies, as well as a multitude of mercenaries, so that his army numbered all told almost fifteen thousand men. Then, seizing Achradine, as it is called, and the Island,[65] which were fortified, and using them as bases, he began a war upon the revolting citizens.

The Syracusans at the outset seized a part of the city which is called Tyche,[66] and operating from there they dispatched ambassadors to Gela, Akragas, and Selinos, and also Himera and the cities of the Siceli in the interior of the island, asking them to come together with all speed and join with them in liberating Syracuse. And since all these cities acceded to this request eagerly and hurriedly dispatched aid, some of them infantry and cavalry and others warships fully equipped for action, in a brief time there was collected a considerable armament with which to aid the Syracusans. Consequently the Syracusans, having made ready their ships and drawn up their army for battle, demonstrated that they were ready to fight to a finish both on land and on sea. Now Thrasyboulos, abandoned as he was by his allies and basing his hopes only upon the mercenaries, was master only of Achradine and the Island, whereas the rest of the city was in the hands of the Syracusans. And after this Thrasyboulos sailed forth with his ships against the enemy, and after suffering defeat in the battle with the loss of numerous triremes, he withdrew with the remaining ships to the Island. Similarly he led forth his army also from Achradine and drew them up for battle in the suburbs, but he suffered defeat and was forced to retire with heavy losses back to Achradine. In the end, giving up hope of maintaining the tyranny, he opened negotiations with the Syracusans, came to an understanding with them, and retired under a truce to Lokroi [in Italy]. The Syracusans, having liberated their native city in this manner, gave permission to the mercenaries to withdraw from Syracuse, and they liberated the other cities, which were either in the hands of tyrants or had garrisons, and re-established democracies in them. From this time the city enjoyed peace and increased greatly in prosperity, and it maintained its democracy for almost sixty years, until the tyranny which was established by Dionysios.[67] But Thrasyboulos, who had taken over a kingship which had been established on so fair a foundation, disgracefully lost his kingdom through his own wickedness, and fleeing to Lokroi he spent the rest of his life there in private station.

THE LAWS OF GORTYN

This long inscription, found at the site of ancient Gortyn in Crete between 1857 and 1884, contains not a comprehensive law code (as it is often loosely called) but a series of ordinances on such varied subjects as slave-owning, rape and assault, adultery, divorce, widow's rights and division of property. These ordinances were prominently displayed to the public by being inscribed on both sides of a low, curved wall. Though inscribed in the older style known as *boustrophedon* ("turning the way an ox plows," i.e. alternate lines read from left to right and right to left), the text is now generally agreed to date from the middle of the fifth century B.C.

Gods:

Whosoever may be likely to contend about a free man or a slave is not to seize him before trial. But if he make seizure, let (the judge) condemn him to (a fine of) ten staters for a free man, five for a slave of whomsoever he does seize and let him give judgment that he release him within three days; but if he do not release him, let (the judge) condemn him to (a fine of) a stater for a free man and a drachma for a slave, for each day until he do release him; and the judge is to decide on oath as to the time; but if he should deny the seizure, unless a witness should testify, the judge is to decide on oath. And if one party contend that he is a free man, the other party that he is a slave, whichever persons testify that he is a free man are to prevail. And if they contend about a slave, each declaring that he is his, the judge is to give judgment according to the witness if a witness testify, but he is to decide on oath if they testify either for both or for neither. After the one in possession has been defeated, he is to release the free man within five days and give back the slave in hand; but if he should not release or give back, let (the judge) give judgment that the (successful party) be entitled, in the case of the free man to fifty staters and a stater for each day until he releases him, in the case of the slave ten staters and a drachma for each day until he gives him back in hand; but at a year's end after the judge has pronounced judgment, the three-fold fines are to be exacted, or less, but not more. As to the time the judge shall decide under oath; but if the slave on whose account a man has been defeated take sanctuary in a temple, (the defeated party) summoning (the successful party) in the presence of two free adult witnesses shall point him out at the temple where he takes refuge, either himself or another for him; and if he do not summon or point out, let him pay what is written; but if he should not give him back at all within the yearly period, he shall in addition pay the single penalties. If he (the defeated party) die while the suit is being tried, he shall pay the single penalty. And if one who is a magistrate make a seizure or another (seize the slave) of one who is a magistrate they are to contend after he resigns, and, if defeated, he shall pay what is written from the day he made the seizure. But one who seizes a man condemned (for debt) or who has mortgaged his person shall be immune from punishment. If a person commits rape on the free man or the free woman, he shall pay one hundred staters; and if on account of an *apetairos*,[68] ten; and if the slave on the free man or the free woman, he shall pay double; and if a free man on a male serf or a female serf, five drachmas; and if a male serf on a male serf or female serf, five staters. If a person should forcibly seduce a slave belonging to the home, he shall pay two staters; but if she has already been seduced, one obol by day, but if in the night, two obols; and the slave shall have preference in the oath. If someone attempt to have intercourse with a free woman who is under the guardianship of a relative, he shall pay ten staters if a witness should testify. If someone be taken in adultery with a free woman in a father's, brother's or the husband's house, he shall pay a hundred staters; but if in another's fifty; and if with the wife of an *apetairos*, ten; but if a slave with a free woman, he shall pay double; and if a slave with a slave, five. Let (the captor) proclaim in the presence of three witnesses to the relatives of the one caught in (the house) that he is to be ransomed within five days; and to the master of the slave in the presence of two witnesses; but if he should not be ransomed himself, it is to be within the power of the captors to deal with him as they may wish; but if anyone should declare that he has been taken by subterfuge, the captor is to swear, in a case involving fifty staters or more, with four others, each calling down solemn curses upon himself, and in the case of an *apetairos* with two others, and in the case of a serf the master and one other, that he took him in adultery and not by subterfuge. And if a husband and wife should be divorced, she is to have her own property which she came with to her husband and half of the produce, if there be any from her own property, and half of whatever she has woven within, whatever there may be, plus five staters if the husband be the cause of the divorce; but if the husband should declare that he is not the cause, the judge is to decide on oath. And if she should carry away anything else belonging to the husband, she shall pay five staters and whatever she may carry away; and let her restore whatever she may have filched; but as regards things which she denies (the judge) shall decree that the woman take an oath of denial by Artemis, before the statue of the Archeress in the Amyklaian temple. And whatever anyone may take away from her after she has made her oath of denial, he shall pay the thing itself plus five staters. If a stranger should help her in packing off, he shall pay ten staters and double the value of whatever the judge swears he helped to pack off. If a man die leaving children, should the wife so desire she may marry, holding her own property and whatever her husband might have given her according to what is written, in the presence of three adult free witnesses; but if she should take away anything belonging to the children, that becomes a matter for trial. And if he should leave her childless, she is to have her own property and half of whatever she has woven within and obtain her portion of the produce that is in the house along with the lawful heirs as well as whatever her husband may have given her as is written; but if she should take away anything else, that becomes a matter for trial. And if a wife should die childless (the husband) is to return her property to the lawful heirs and the half of whatever she has woven within and the half of the produce, if it be from her own property. If the husband or wife wish to make payments for porterage, (these should be) either clothing or twelve staters or something of the value of twelve staters, but not more. If a female serf be separated from a serf while he is alive or in case of his death, she is to have her own property; but if she should carry away anything else, that becomes a matter for trial. If a wife who is separated (by divorce) should bear a child, (they) are to bring it to the husband at his house in the presence of three witnesses; and if he should not receive it, the child shall be in the mother's power either to rear or expose; and the relatives and witnesses shall have preference in the oath as to whether they brought it. And if a female serf should bear a child while separated, (they) are to bring it to the master of the man who married her in the presence of two witnesses.

And if he do not receive it, the child shall be in the power of the master of the female serf; but if she should marry the same man again before the end of the year, the child shall be in the power of the master of the male serf, and the one who brought it and the witnesses shall have preference in the oath. If a woman separated (by divorce) should expose her child before presenting it as is written, if she is convicted, she shall pay, for a free child, fifty staters, for a slave, twenty-five. And if the man should have no house to which she shall bring it or she do not see him, there is to be no penalty if she should expose the child. If a female serf who is unmarried should conceive and bear, the child shall be in the power of the master of her father; but in case the father should not be living, it shall be in the power of the masters of her brothers. The father shall be in control of the children and the division of the property and the mother of her own property. So long as they are living there is no necessity to make a division; but if anyone should be fined, the one fined shall have his share apportioned to him as is written. And in case (the father) should die, the city houses and whatever there is in those houses in which a serf living in the country does not reside, and the cattle, small and large, which do not belong to a serf, shall belong to the sons; but all the rest of the property shall be fairly divided and the sons, no matter how many shall each receive two parts, while the daughters, no matter how many, shall each receive one part. The mother's property too, in case she dies, shall be divided in the same way as is prescribed for the father's; but if there should be no property except the house, the daughters shall receive their share as is prescribed. And if the father, while living, should wish to give to the married daughter, let him give according to what is prescribed, but not more. Any (daughter) to whom he gave or pledged before shall have these things, but shall obtain nothing besides from the paternal property.

Whatever woman has no property either by gift from father or brother or by pledge or by inheritance . . . such women are to obtain their portion; but there shall be no ground for action against previous female beneficiaries. When a man or a woman dies, if there be children or children's children or children's children's children, they are to have the property. And if there be none of these, but brothers of the deceased and brothers' children or brothers' children's children, they are to have the property. And if there be none of these, but sisters of the deceased and sisters' children or sisters' children's children, they are to have the property. And if there be none of these, they are to take it up, to whom it may fall as source of the property. And if there should be no kinsmen, those of the household comprising the heirs are to have the property. And if some of the next-of-kin wish to divide the property while others do not, the judge shall decree that all the property shall be in the power of those who wish to divide until they divide it. And if anyone enters in by force or drives or carries off anything once the judge has made his decision, he shall pay ten staters and double the value of the piece of property. So far as livestock, produce, clothing, ornaments and movable property are concerned, if they do not wish to make a division, the judge shall decide under oath with reference to the pleas. And if, when dividing the property, they cannot agree about the division, they shall offer the property for sale; and, having sold it to him who offers most, let each of them take his share of the values. And when they are dividing the property, three or more adult free witnesses are to be present.

Should he give to a daughter, the same procedure is to be followed. As long as the father lives, no one shall offer to purchase any of the paternal property from a son nor take out a mortgage on it; but whatever (the son) himself may have acquired or inherited, let him sell, if he wishes. Nor shall the father sell or mortgage the possessions of his children, whatever they have themselves acquired or inherited. Nor shall the husband sell or pledge those of his wife, nor the son those of his mother. And if anyone should purchase or take on mortgage or accept a promise otherwise than is written in these writings, the property shall be in the power of the mother and the wife, and the one who sold or mortgaged or promised shall pay two-fold to the one who bought or accepted the mortgage or the promise and, if there be any other damage besides, the simple value; but in matters of previous date there shall be no ground for action. If, however, the defendant should maintain, with reference to the matter about which they contend, that it is not in the power of the mother or the wife, the action shall be brought where it belongs, before the judge where it is prescribed for each case. If a mother die leaving children, the father is to be in control of the mother's property, but he shall not sell or mortgage unless the children consent and are of age; but if anyone should otherwise purchase or take on mortgage, the property shall be in the power of the children and the seller or mortgagor shall pay twofold the value to the purchaser or mortgagee and, if there be any other damage besides, the simple value. And, if he should marry another woman, the children are to be in control of the mother's property. If anyone, bound by necessity, should get a man gone away to a strange place set free from a foreign city at his own request, he shall be in the power of the one who ransomed him until he pay what is due; but if they do not agree about the amount or on the ground that he did not request to be set free, the judge is to decide on oath with reference to the pleas . . . (If the slave) goes to a free woman and marries her, their children shall be free; but if the free woman goes to the slave, their children shall be slaves. And if free and slave children should be born of the same mother, in a case where the mother dies, if there is property, the free children are to have it; but if there should be no free children born of her, the heirs are to take it over. If someone has bought a slave from the marketplace and has not terminated the agreement within sixty days, the one who has acquired him shall be liable, if (the slave) has done any wrong before or after (the purchase). The heiress is to be married to the brother of her father, the oldest of those living. And, if there be more heiresses and brothers of the father, they are to be married to the next oldest. And if there should be no brothers of the father, but sons of the brothers, she is to be married to that one (who is the son) of the oldest. And if there should be more heiresses and sons of brothers, they are to be married to the next after the son of the oldest. The groom-elect is to have one heiress and not more. As long as the groom-elect or the heiress is too young to marry, the heiress is to have the house, if there is one, and the groom-elect is to obtain half the revenue from everything; but if the groom-elect should not wish to marry the heiress, though they are both of an age to marry, on the grounds that he is still a minor, all the property and the produce shall be at the disposal of the heiress until he does marry her; but if the groom-elect, now an adult, should not wish to marry the heiress who is of an age and willing to be married to him, the relatives of the heiress are to bring the matter to court and the judge is to order the marriage to take place within two months. And if he should not marry her as written, the heiress, holding all the property, is to marry the next in succession, if there be another; but if there be no groom-elect, she is to be married to whomsoever she wishes of those who ask from the tribe. And if the heiress, though of an age to marry, should not wish to be married to the groom-elect, or the groom-elect be too young and the heiress be unwilling to wait, the heiress is to have a house, if there be one in the city, besides whatever may be in that house, and, obtaining half a share of the rest, she is to be married to another, whomsoever she may wish of those who ask from the tribe; but she is to give a share of the property to that one (i.e. to the rejected groom-elect). And if there should not be kinsmen of the heiress as is defined, she may hold all of the property and be married to whomsoever she may wish from the tribe. And if no one from the tribe should wish to marry her, the relatives of the heiress are to proclaim throughout the tribe: "Does no one wish to marry her?" And if anyone should marry her, (it should be) within thirty days from the time they made the proclamation; but if not, she is to be married to another, whomsoever she can. And if a woman becomes an heiress after her father or brother has given her (in marriage), if she should not wish to remain married to the one to whom they gave her, although he be willing, if she has borne children, she may be married to another of the tribe, dividing the property as is prescribed; but if there should be no children, she is to be married to the groom-elect, if there be one, and take all the property; and if there is not, as is prescribed. If a husband should die leaving children to an heiress, let her be married to whomsoever of the tribe she can, if she should so wish, but without any compulsion; but if the deceased should leave no children behind, she is to be married to the groom-elect as is prescribed. And if the man who has the right to marry the heiress should not be at home, and the heiress should be of marriageable age, let her be married to the (next) groom-elect as is prescribed. Now an heiress is one who has no father or brother from the same father. And as long as she is not of an age to marry, her father's brothers are to be responsible for the administration of the property, while she takes half a share of the produce; but if there should be no groom-elect while she is not of an age to marry, the heiress is to have charge of the property and the produce and is to be brought up with her mother as long as she is not of an age to marry; and if there should be no mother, she is to be brought up with her mother's brothers. Now if anyone should marry the heiress otherwise than is prescribed, the lawful heirs are to lay information before a magistrate. If someone owing money should leave behind an heiress, she either personally or through her paternal and maternal relatives shall mortgage or sell to the value of the debt, and the purchase and mortgage shall be legal. And if anyone should otherwise buy or take on mortgage the property of the heiress, the property shall be at the disposal of the heiress, and the seller or mortgagor, if he be convicted, shall pay double to the buyer or mortgagee, and if there is any other damage he shall pay the simple value in addition, since the inscription of this law, but there shall be no liability in matters of previous date; but if the defendant should maintain, with reference to the matter about which they contend, that it does not belong to the heiress, let the judge decide under oath. And if he should win his case that it does not belong to the heiress, action should be brought where it is prescribed for each case. If one dies who has gone surety or has lost a suit or owes money given as security or has been involved in fraud(?) or has made a promise(?) or another (be in like relationship) to him, one must bring suit against that person before the end of the year; and let the judge give his decision according to the testimony. If the suit be with reference to a judgment won, the judge and the recorder, if alive and a citizen, and the heirs as witnesses (shall testify), but in the case of surety and money given as securities and fraud(?) and promise(?), the heirs as witnesses shall testify. And after they have testified, let (the judge) decree that (the plaintiff), when he has taken oath himself along with the witnesses, have judgment for the simple amount. If a son has gone surety, while his father is living, he and the property which he possesses shall be subject to fine. If one has formed a partnership with another for a mercantile venture, in case he does not pay back the one who has contributed to the venture, if witnesses who are of age should testify — three in a case of a hundred staters or more, two in a case of less down to ten staters, one for still less — let (the judge) decide according to the testimony; but if witnesses should not testify, in case the contracting party comes, whichever course the complainant demands, either to deny an oath or . . .

A son may give to a mother or a husband to a wife one hundred staters or less, but not more. And if he should give more, the heirs are to keep the property if they wish, once they have handed over the money. If anyone owing money or being the loser in a suit or while a suit is being tried should give anything away, the gift shall be invalid, if the rest of the property should not be equal to the obligation. No one shall offer to buy a man while pledged until the mortgagor release him, nor one who is the subject of legal process, nor accept him (in payment) nor accept him (in pledge) nor take him in mortgage. And if anyone does any of these things, it shall be invalid, if two witnesses should testify. Adoption may be made from whatever source anyone wishes. And the declaration of adoption shall be made in the place of assembly when the citizens are gathered, from the stone from which proclamations are made. And let the adopter give to his social group a sacrificial victim and a measure of wine. And if he (the adopted person) should receive all the property and there should be no legitimate children besides, he must fulfil all the obligations of the adopter towards gods and men and receive as is written for legitimate children; but if he should not be willing to fulfil these obligations as is written, the next-of-kin shall have the property. And if there should be legitimate children of the adopter, the adopted son shall receive with the males just as females receive from their brothers; and if there should be no males, but females, the adopted son is to have an equal share and it shall not be incumbent upon him to pay the obligations of the adopter and accept the property which the adopter leaves; for the adopted son is not to take possession of more (than the females); but if the adopted son should die without leaving legitimate children, the property is to revert to the heirs of the adopter. And if the adopter wishes, he may renounce (the adopted son) in the place of assembly when the citizens are gathered, from the stone from which proclamations are made; and he shall deposit ten staters with the court, and the secretary (of the magistrates) who is concerned with strangers shall pay it to the person renounced; but a woman shall not adopt nor a person under puberty. And these regulations shall be followed from the time of the inscription of this law; but as regards matters of previous date, in whatever way one hold (property), whether by adoption or from an adopted son, there shall still be no liability. Anyone may at any time receive a man if any person seize him before trial. Whatever it is written that he shall give judgment upon, either according to witnesses or under oath of denial, the judge is to give judgment as is written; but in other matters he shall decide under oath according to the pleas. If a person should die owing money or having lost a suit, if those to whom it falls to receive the property should wish to pay the fine on his behalf and the money to those to whom he may owe it, they are to have the property; but if they do not so wish, the property shall belong to those who won the suit or those to whom he owes money, and the heirs shall not be liable to any further fine; and the paternal property shall be laid under obligation for the father's debts, the maternal for the mother's. If a judge has decreed an oath in a case where a wife is divorced from her husband, let her take the oath of denial of whatever one charges within twenty days in the presence of the judge; and let the initiator of the suit make his denunciation to the woman and the judge and the secretary (of the court) on the fourth day beforehand in the presence of a witness who has been adult for fifteen years or more. If a son has given property to his mother or a husband to his wife in the way prescribed before these regulations, there shall be no liability; but henceforth gifts shall be made as here prescribed. If there are no judges in the affairs of orphans, the heiresses shall be treated according to these regulations so long as they are not of marriageable age. And where the heiress, in default of a groom-elect or of judges in the affairs of orphans, is brought up with her mother, the paternal and maternal relatives, those who have been nominated, shall administer the property and the income to the best of their ability until she is married. And she is to be married when twelve years of age or older.

OSTRACISM
A. Diodoros of Sicily 11.54-55 and 87
B. Philochoros, fragment 30

Though it existed in a number of Greek cities, ostracism — condemnation to honorable exile for a fixed term, without loss of citizenship or property — is best known to us as it was practiced at Athens. Introduced there by Kleisthenes as a defense against a renascence of tyranny, ostracism was applied for the first time in 487 B.C. Close to two thousand sherds (*ostraka* in Greek), bearing the names of more than sixty different individuals, have been found in the excavations of the Athenian agora and the

Kerameikos area. Ostracism fell into disrepute and was discontinued at Athens after 417 B.C.: in that year or soon after, the major political groups, each fearing that its leader would be ostracized, joined forces to victimize a third party. Similar collusion is exemplified by a group of 191 ostraka bearing the name of Themistokles: the entire group was inscribed by only fourteen different hands — obviously they were prepared in advance and distributed to partisans to cast as ballots.

Philochoros, who lived in the third century B.C., was the most prominent of a group known as Atthidographers, or writers of Athenian history. An account of ostracism may also be found in Plutarch's *Life of Aristeides,* chapter 7.

A

But afterwards those who feared the eminence he [Themistokles] enjoyed, and others who were envious of his glory forgot his services to the state, and began to exert themselves to diminish his power and to lower his presumption. First of all they removed him from Athens, employing against him what is called ostracism, an institution which was adopted in Athens after the overthrow of the tyranny of Peisistratos and his sons; and the law was as follows. Each citizen wrote on a piece of pottery (*ostrakon*) the name of the man who in his opinion had the greatest power to destroy the democracy; and the man who got the largest number of ostraca was obliged by the law to go into exile from his native land for a period of ten years. The Athenians, it appears, passed such a law, not for the purpose of punishing wrongdoing, but in order to lower through exile the presumption of men who had risen too high. Now Themistokles, having been ostracized in the manner we have described, fled as an exile from his native city to Argos . . .

Now among the Athenians each citizen was required to write on a potsherd (*ostrakon*) the name of the man who, in his opinion, was most able through his influence to tyrannize over his fellow citizens; but among the Syracusans the name of the most influential citizen had to be written on an olive leaf, and when the leaves were counted, the man who received the largest number of leaves had to go into exile for five years. For by this means they thought that they would humble the arrogance of the most powerful men in these two cities; for, speaking generally, they were not exacting from violators of the law a punishment for a crime committed, but were effecting a diminution of the influence and growing power of the men in question. Now while the Athenians called this kind of legislation ostracism, from the way it was done, the Syracusans used the name petalism. This law remained in force among the Athenians for a long time, but among the Syracusans it was soon repealed for the following reasons. Since the most influential men were being sent into exile, the most respectable citizens and such as had it in their power, by reason of their personal high character, to effect many reforms in the affairs of the commonwealth were taking no part in public affairs, but consistently remained in private life because of their fear of the law, attending to their personal fortunes and leaning towards a life of luxury; whereas it was the basest citizens and such as excelled in effrontery who were giving their attention to public affairs and inciting the masses to disorder and revolution. Consequently, since factional quarrels were again arising and the masses were turning to wrangling, the city fell back into continuous and serious disorders. For a multitude of demagogues and sycophants was arising, the youth were cultivating cleverness in oratory, and, in a word, many were exchanging the ancient and sober way of life for the ignoble pursuits; wealth was increasing because of the peace, but there was little if any concern for concord and honest conduct. As a result the Syracusans changed their minds and repealed the law of petalism, having used it only a short while.

B

Banishment by ostracism was carried out as follows. Before the eighth prytany the assembly took a preliminary vote on whether it saw fit to proceed to the ostracon. When it so decreed, the agora was fenced with boards and ten entrances were left open through which they entered and deposited their ostraca by tribes, concealing the inscription; the nine archons and the council presided over the proceedings. When the count was taken, anyone who received more and not less than 6,000 had to pay the penalty, make contractual arrangements about his property, and within ten days go into exile from the city for ten years, enjoying his revenues but no coming closer (to Athens) than Cape Geraios on Euboia. The only undistinguished figure to be ostracized was

Hyperbolos — on account of the depravity of his ways, not through suspicion of tyranny; this marked the end of the custom legislated by Kleisthenes when he deposed the tyrants, as a way of casting out their friends with them.[69]

DECREE OF BANISHMENT
Meiggs-Lewis 43

In this decree of ca. 443 B.C. the city of Miletos condemns two families to perpetual and hereditary banishment, presumably because they attempted by coup d'état to establish a tyranny. The small amounts of the reward and fines suggest that Miletos was not very prosperous at this time.

... sons of Nympharetos, and Alkimos and Kresophontes sons of Stratonax, themselves and their descendants, are condemned for murder to exile, and whoever kills anyone of them shall receive a hundred staters from the property of Nympharetos; the magistrates of the month when the killers come forward shall pay the money, and if not they themselves shall be fined (that amount). If they fall into the city's power they shall be put to death by the magistrates of the month in which they are seized; if they do not put them to death they shall each be fined fifty staters; if the chief magistrate does not put the motion he shall be fined a hundred staters and the incoming magistracy shall in turn act according to this decree; if not they shall pay the same penalty.

PRESERVING THE POLITICAL STATUS QUO:
REWARDS FOR INFORMERS
Meiggs-Lewis 83

This inscription contains two laws tentatively assignable to the oligarchy that came to power in the island of Thasos in 411 B.C. The second law is dated at least seventeen months after the first.

Whoever denounces an uprising being plotted against Thasos and shows his information to be true, shall receive a thousand staters[70] from the city; if a slave denounces, he shall also be free. If more than one denounce, three hundred men shall judge and decide the issue.[71] If any one of the participants (in the plot) denounces, he shall receive the money and there shall be no accusation sworn against him, nor any indictment, sacred or secular, in this matter, nor shall he be under the curse — excepting, however, the one having initiated the plot. Effective the twenty-ninth of Apatourion in the archonship of Akryptos, Aleximachos and Dexiades.

Whoever in the colonies denounces an uprising being plotted — i.e. someone betraying the city of Thasos or of the colony — and shows his information to be true, shall receive two hundred staters from the city; if the estate of the revolter is worth more than two hundred staters, he shall receive four hundred staters from the city; if a slave denounces, he shall receive the money and shall be free. If more than one denounce, three hundred men shall judge and decide the issue. If any one of the participants (in the plot) denounces, he shall receive the money and there shall be no accusation sworn against him, nor any indictment, sacred or secular, in this matter, nor shall he be under the curse — excepting, however, the one having initiated the plot. Effective date of this ordinance is the third of Galaxion in the archonship of Phanodikos, Antiphanes and Ktesillos.

FUNERAL REGULATIONS
Syll. 1218

Solon in Athens and other eminent lawgivers elsewhere are said to have passed sumptuary legislation limiting the ostentation of banquets, funerals and other evidences of conspicuous consumption. The following funerary law from the city of Ioulis on the island of Keos is a late fifth-century reinscription of earlier enactments.

The laws concerning the departed.
The dead shall be buried as follows: in three or fewer white

cloths — i.e. a spread, a shroud and a coverlet — the three worth not over a hundred drachmas. They shall carry him out on a simply-wrought bed and shall not cover the bier with the cloths. They shall take to the tomb not more than three choes of wine and not more than one chous of olive oil, and they shall carry away the (empty) jars. They shall carry the corpse covered,[72] in silence all the way to the tomb. They shall perform the pre-burial sacrifice according to ancestral custom. They shall carry home from the tomb the bed and the spreads.

On the following day a free man shall sprinkle first the house with sea water, and then all the rooms with hyssop. When it has been sprinkled throughout, the house shall be cleansed and they shall offer sacrifices upon the hearth.

The women who go to the funeral shall not go away from the tomb before the men.

They shall not hold monthly services for the dead.

They shall not place a cup beneath the bed, nor pour out the water, nor carry the sweepings to the tomb.

Wherever a person dies, after the bed is carried out no women shall go to the house except those polluted (by the death); those polluted are mother, wife, sisters and daughters, in addition to these not more than five women, namely children of daughters and cousins, and no one else. The polluted shall be cleansed by washing . . . in poured water.

[The rest is lost.]

WATER RIGHTS
Syll. 1183

This fifth-century inscription from Gortyn illustrates the efforts of Greek cities to husband that precious agricultural commodity, water.

Gods. Anyone diverting water from the middle of the river to irrigate his own property shall do so without penalty, but he shall leave as much water as the bridge in the agora spans or more, but not less.

A FAMOUS ATHLETE
Inschriften von Olympia 153

Fragments of a statue base found at Olympia in 1877 are inscribed with a list of the victories won by an athlete named Dorieus at the four panhellenic games (which are inscribed in their order of fame and importance: Olympic, Delphic [or Pythian], Isthmian and Nemean). According to Pausanias (*Description of Greece* 6.7.1) Dorieus won the pankration at Olympia on three successive occasions, and according to Thucydides (3.8) the second of those victories came in 428 B.C. Since seven victories are recorded at the Isthmian and Nemean games (Pausanias 6.7.4 says eight for the Isthmian), it follows that Dorieus' victorious career extended over at least 26 years. Only one comparable athletic career is known to us from the fifth century B.C., that of Theagenes of Thasos, with nine Nemean and ten Isthmian victories.

As indicated above, Dorieus' fame was such that he was spoken of in ancient literature, notably Xenophon's *Hellenic History* and Pausanias' *Description of Greece*. From these we learn that Dorieus fought in the Peloponnesian War on the Spartan side and was captured by the Athenians, who then released him without ransom because of his athletic renown.

Dorieus son of Diagoras, of Rhodes

At Olympia pankration[73]	At the Isthmos boxing
At Olympia pankration	At the Isthmos boxing
At Olympia pankration	At the Isthmos —[75]
At Delphi boxing	At the Isthmos —[75]
At Delphi boxing	At Nemea boxing
At Delphi boxing, effortlessly[74]	At Nemea boxing
At the Isthmos boxing	At Nemea boxing
At the Isthmos boxing	At Nemea boxing
At the Isthmos boxing and pankration	At Nemea boxing
	At Nemea boxing
	At Nemea boxing

A RECORD OF MANUMISSION
Syll. 1204

Found on Mt. Kotylon, this bronze tablet of the fifth century B.C. contains an early example of the manumission of slaves.

God, fortune. Klenis has set free Komaithon, Elythron, Ombria and Choirothyon. If anyone lays a hand on them all his property shall be consecrated to Apollo of Bassai, to Pan Sinoeis, to Artemis of Kotylon and to (Artemis) Orthasia.

A FAITH CURE
Inschriften von Olympia 267

On a statue base found in 1879 in the ruins of the Hera temple, this inscription of ca. 460 B.C. explains the many dedications of Mikynthos at Olympia. Pausanias, reporting that these statues were still visible in the second century A.D., writes (*Description of Greece* 5.26.5), "The inscriptions on the thank offerings give Choiros as the name of Mikynthos' father, and the Greek cities of Rhegion and Messene on the strait as his fatherland. The inscriptions say that he dwelt in Tegea, and he dedicated the thank offerings at Olympia in fulfillment of a vow for the recovery of a son who had fallen ill of a wasting disease." On the basis of this text the inscription, of which only the right-hand third is extant, may be restored as follows.

Mikynthos son of Choiros, native of Rhegion and Messene dwelling in Tegea, dedicated these statues to all the gods and all the goddesses. His son was ill of a wasting disease, and after spending a substantial fortune on doctors he came to Olympia and then prayed . . .
[The rest is lost.]

FOOTNOTES

1. For the missing word here rendered as "residents" the reading "kinsmen" has also been proposed.

2. Perhaps something like, "shall [approve the arms of the men under arms. This was decreed] in the council."

3. These verses may be part of a longer poem that was sung in Sparta at the shrine of the fallen.

4. Sparta's name is first because the Spartans ordered the inscription. As Thucydides tells it (1.32.2-3), "On the tripod at Delphi which the Greeks dedicated as first fruits of the spoils from the Persians . . . the Spartans . . . inscribed by name all the cities which together had destroyed the barbarian and had erected the dedicatory offering."

5. The law apparently stipulated other commodities as well, but they were omitted from this citation as irrelevant to the instant case.

6. When the tribute was due.

7. That is, three citizens to guard the construction site, as distinct from the public slaves ("Scythian archers") who were the ordinary policemen of Athens in the fifth century B.C.

8. At Histiaia in Euboia Athenian prisoners had been massacred. In retaliation Athens drove out the people of that city and settled Athenian colonists on their land.

9. Embassies from allied states had frequently cooled their heels for long periods in Athens.

10. A neighboring city in Euboia. An extant fragment of an inscription confirms that the oath imposed on Eretria was identical with that imposed on Chalkis.

11. The seer who accompanied the Athenian army to Euboia.

12. Obviously a treasurer, perhaps a Hellenotamias.

13. The "treasurers of the goddess" actually numbered more than seven. Why only these are named is not clear.

14. I.e., this is the fourteenth year of these building accounts.

15. "A supply of Lampsakene and Kyzikene electrum staters which had remained untouched since they were given to the first year's board. Presumably contractors and workmen wanted their wages in good Attic coin" — Meiggs-Lewis p. 164.

16. "Ivory [is here] three times cheaper than in fourth-century Delphi; no doubt the [commissioners] were selling off waste" — Meiggs-Lewis p. 163.

17. This figure, partly preserved, ran into the hundreds and probably into the thousands.

18. By this date the sculptors were presumably completing the figures of the pediments.

19. The figure, only partly preserved, was over 1800.

20. Since treaty oaths were reciprocal (cf. e.g. p. 27), the missing portion must have, *inter alia*, repeated the oath for Rhegion. In Meiggs-Lewis 64 the Leontinians repeat verbatim the oath sworn by the Athenians.

21. "The priestesses of Apollo at Delphi often ordered neglectful cities to contribute shares of their harvests" (Isokrates, *Panegyrikos* 31).

22. The medimnos was a dry measure, equivalent to ca. 1 1/2 bushels.

23. Flour made from the choicest wheat and barley, and used for ceremonial purposes.

24. One of two families (the other was named Kerykes) traditionally in charge of the rites at Eleusis. According to legend their ancestor Eumolpos founded the mysteries there.

25. "The good counselor," a euphemistic designation for divinity associated with several Greek deities, notably those of Eleusis.

26. Minor treasury officials.

27. The name of two salt-water inlets, one coming near the city, the other remaining closer to the sea.

28. This temple, built in the age of Peisistratos, had been burned by the Persians in the invasion of 480 B.C.

29. These (as we learn from chapter 119.2) were Corinth, Sikyon, Megara and Epidauros.

30. The Peloponnesian name for Pylos; Bouphras and Tomeus are otherwise unknown.

31. Athens had made Kythera tributary in 424 B.C.

32. Presumably Atalante is meant: cf. p. 26.

33. Up to this point Thucydides quotes the preamble of the actual decree; the rest is paraphrase.

34. The day after the City Dionysia at which Aristophanes' *Clouds* was awarded second or third prize.

35. This reduces the tribute to what it was before it was more than doubled, to pay for the war, in the assessment of 425/4 B.C.: cf. p. 9.

36. These clauses on the return of places and persons were not carried out in good faith, occasioning many mutual recriminations (some of which are reported by Thucydides 5.35-46).

37. This clause amounts to acceptance of the *fait accompli*: e.g. the women and children of Torone had already been sold into slavery and the men had been sent to Athens pending the turn of events.

38. It is noteworthy that this provision is not made reciprocal, since there was no such threat at Athens comparable to that of the helots at Sparta.

39. The sums of money were given item by item in a column to the left, of which faint traces remain.

40. In the inventory of 401/0 B.C. this item is described more fully as "a gold crown which the Nike on the hand of the gold statue has on her head." The "gold statue" is, of course, Pheidias' chryselephantine statue of Athena.

41. The name of a slave.

42. Kephisodoros' wealth was invested in slaves: as a metic he was disbarred from owning real estate.

43. This caption and all of the first column are missing. The identification of the property as that of Alkibiades is established by a remark in the lexicon compiled by the grammarian Pollux in the second century A.D.

44. One of a group in the Four Hundred who tried to deliver Athens over to Sparta. He was murdered, and his bones were strewn beyond the borders. For further details see *Cambridge Ancient History* Vol. 5, pp. 336-38.

45. The son of the famous Perikles and Aspasia, he had been granted Athenian citizenship.

46. Probably "a measure of poor relief instituted by the state during the closing years of the Peloponnesian War, when the loss of Euboea and the Spartan occupation of Decelea brought widespread ruin to Athenian citizens" — Meiggs-Lewis p. 260.

47. The son of Nikias.

48. The total amount must have been in the neighborhood of 180 talents.

49. The unfinished work is listed first, and the extant inscription breaks off before that roster is completed.

50. The temple of Kekrops, for whom see note 54.

51. The famous Porch of the Maidens, or Karyatid Porch.

52. Pandrosos was the daughter of Kekrops (see note 54).

53. The black stone, which contrasted with the Pentelic marble, came from Eleusis.

54. The Athenians, so called from their mythical king Kekrops; cf. note 50.

55. A decree was normally proposed by a single individual. This unique expression emphasizes the unanimity of the movers of this decree.

56. In 412 B.C., when democracy was restored at Samos.

57. A manifestation of his newly acquired citizenship.

58. A further mark of honor; subject states were usually required to pay for the stele to be erected at Athens: cf. pp. 16, 17.

59. Which board of ten is meant is not clear. Since the reference is obviously to the Thirty Tyrants and certain officials who served under them, perhaps the manuscript text is faulty and Aristotle originally wrote "the Thirty, the Ten former governors of the Peiraieus, and the Eleven [superintendents of the prison]."

60. A detailed commentary on this law and on the text as here given will be found in C. Hignett, *A History of the Athenian Constitution* (Oxford, 1952), pp. 300-303.

61. Statues of the legendary heroes after whom the Athenian tribes and demes were named.

62. For example, the oaths sworn in instituting the recent oligarchies.

63. Inscribed lists of "king's benefactors" were displayed at court. These are mentioned in Herodotos (8.85) and in the Book of Esther (chap. 6).

64. I.e. through his oracles.

65. Achradinê was the height north of the city and the Island is Ortygia, on which the palace and public buildings were located.

66. This section adjoined Achradinê on the west.

67. In 406 B.C.

68. One not a member of any of the citizen social groups *(hetaireiai)*.

69. The scholia on Aristophanes' *Knights* verse 855 repeat the first part of the Philochoros text and add: "Not only Athens voted ostracism, but also Argos, Miletos and Megara. Practically all the most accomplished men were ostracized, Aristeides, Kimon, Themistokles, Thucydides, Alkibiades."

70. Equivalent to 1600 Athenian drachmas.

71. I.e. the issue of who is to receive the reward.

72. To avoid polluting the city and the light of day.

73. A combined boxing-wrestling contest.

74. A special distinction, apparently awarded only rarely. Literally the Greek word means "without raising dust," i.e. there was no real contest, it was a pushover.

75. These spaces are vacant in the inscription.

GLOSSARY OF NAMES AND TECHNICAL TERMS

agora: a market place, the business center of a Greek city.

akroterion: an ornament placed at an angle of a pediment.

amphora: a two-handled vase; also a liquid measure, the standard amphora holding ca. 6 gallons.

archon: title of a high official in many Greek cities. In Athens a board of nine archons was elected by lot annually and the year was identified by the name of one of them, styled *archon eponymos.*

boule: a council; at Athens the council of 500 (50 from each tribe) elected by lot annually.

choregia: an obligation, assigned in rotation to the wealthiest Athenian citizens, to serve as *choregos,* i.e. to train and outfit a chorus for a dithyramb (lyric) or a dramatic festival.

chous (plural *choes*): a liquid measure, ca. 3 quarts.

cleruchy: an Athenian colony whose members (cleruchs, so called from the land allotment — *kleros* — given them) retained their original citizenship, serving in effect as an Athenian garrison abroad.

demarch: chief official of an Athenian deme.

deme: one of a hundred or so geographical districts into which Attika was divided.

Dionysia: festivals in honor of the god Dionysos. The Great (or City) Dionysia, celebrated at Athens in late winter or early spring, devoted three days to a contest in which tragic and comic poets presented their new works before the public.

drachma: a weight and a silver coin, the basic Greek monetary unit, divided into 6 obols.

Eleven: an Athenian commission in charge of arrests, imprisonment and execution.

ephors: literally, "overseers": a board of five, elected annually at Sparta. Combining executive and judicial powers, they exercised a *de facto* control of the state.

Hellanodikai: judges and administrators of the Olympic games.

Hellenotamiai (singular *Hellenotamias*): Athenian treasurers of the tribute of the Delian confederacy.

Herakleidai: sons of Herakles, in Dorian legend conquerors of the Peloponnese.

Hyakinthia: games at Sparta in honor of the god (of pre-Hellenic origin) Hyakinthos.

metic: a resident alien at Athens. Attracted by the advantages of Athens' supremacy, many metics built up prosperous businesses there, while others were important in the intellectual life of the city.

mina: a weight and monetary unit = 100 drachmas.

nomothetai: literally, "lawgivers": a body of 500 appointed in 403/2 B.C., after the overthrow of the Thirty, to prepare an up-to-date revision of the essential laws of the democracy.

obol: a minor monetary unit; 6 obols = 1 drachma.

Olympiad: the period of four years between Olympic games, used from ca. 300 B.C. on as a method of dating historical events reckoning from 776 B.C., the year in which the Greeks began to keep a continuous record of victors at the pan-hellenic festivals.

paidagogos: a slave bodyguard who attended his master's child to and from school.

Panathenaia: the chief festival at Athens in honor of Athena, including music and poetry as well as athletic contests. It was held in summer, the Greater Panathenaia for eight days in the third year of each Olympiad, the Lesser Panathenaia for two days in the other years.

peltast: a light-armed soldier, so called from the small round shield (*pelte*) that he carried.

polemarch: the title, surviving from earlier times, borne by one of the Athenian archons.

Prometheia: a festival in honor of Prometheus, at which torch races were a symbolic feature.

prytanis (plural *prytaneis*): The fifty members of each tribe in the Athenian *boule* (council of 500) served as a kind of executive committee for one-tenth of the year, in an order determined by lot; a person so serving was a prytanis, the period of service a prytany and the prytaneion was the place where they worked and dined. Each day one of their number was chosen by lot to be chairman, and he also presided over any meeting of the council or assembly that might be held on that day.

talent: a weight (= 83 1/2 pounds) and monetary unit = 60 minas = 6,000 drachmas.

Thargelia: the principal festival of Apollo at Athens, celebrated in the spring and featuring a lyrical competition.

thesmothetai: six of the annual archons at Athens, exercising judicial functions.

Thirty: the oligarchic government installed at Athens at the end of the Peloponnesian War under the protection of a Spartan garrison. After a reign of terror of several months they were ousted by a band of democratic exiles led by Thrasyboulos.

thetes: the lowest of the four census classes at Athens. They were mostly laborers, and in war time served in the fleet with equipment provided by the state.

trierarchy: an obligation, assigned in rotation to the wealthiest Athenian citizens, to serve as trierarch, i.e. to captain a trireme for a year, maintaining and repairing it at his own expense.

zeugitai: the third (in descending order) of the four census classes at Athens. They were mostly farmers and artisans, and in war time served in the infantry, each man supplying his own arms.

SELECT BIBLIOGRAPHY

The literature on Greece — especially Athens — in the fifth century B.C. is enormous. Given below is a list of significant books and articles in English published during the last ten years. These will generally provide necessary references to earlier works. Bibliographies of important work published prior to 1926 or 1927 will be found in the relevant volumes of the Cambridge Ancient History, published in those years: Vol. 4, *Persia and the West*, Vol. 5, *Athens*.

M. Amit, *Athens and the Sea. A Study in Athenian Sea-Power*, Brussels, 1965.

A. Andrewes, "The Government of Classical Sparta," in *Ancient Society and Institutions: Studies Presented to Victor Ehrenberg*, New York, 1967, pp. 1-20.

——, *The Greeks*, London, 1967.

P.D. Arnott, *An Introduction to the Greek World*, London, 1967.

F.A.G. Beck, *Greek Education 450-350 B.C.*, London, 1964.

P.A. Brunt, "Athenian Settlements Abroad in the Fifth Century B.C.," in *Ancient Society and Institutions*, New York, 1967, pp. 71-92.

J.J. Buchanan, *Theorika: A Study of Monetary Distributions to the Athenian Citizenry during the Fifth and Fourth Centuries B.C.*, New York, 1962.

A.M. Burford, "The Economics of Greek Temple Building," in *Proceedings of the Cambridge Philological Society* 11, 1965, pp. 21-34.

A.R. Burn, *Persia and the Greeks. The Defence of the West, c. 546-478 B.C.* London, 1962.

F. Chamoux, *The Civilization of Greece*, London, 1965.

J.N. Clastner, *Athenian Democracy: Triumph or Travesty?* New York, 1967.

J.A. Davison, "Aeschylus and Athenian Politics," in *Ancient Society and Institutions,* New York, 1967, pp. 93-107.

G.E.M. de Ste. Croix, "Notes on Jurisdiction in the Athenian Empire," in *Classical Quarterly* 11, 1961, pp. 94-112 and 268-80.

V. Ehrenberg, *From Solon to Socrates: Greek History and Civilization during the Sixth and Fifth Centuries B.C.,* London, 1968.

——, *The Greek State,* 2nd ed, London, 1969.

C.W.J. Eliot, *Coastal Demes of Attica, A Study of the Policy of Kleisthenes.* Toronto, 1962 (Phoenix Supplement 5).

J.A.S. Evans, "The Final Problem at Thermopylae," in *Greek, Roman and Byzantine Studies* 5, 1964, pp. 231-37.

M.I. Finley, *The Ancient Greeks,* London, 1963.

R. Flacelière, *Daily Life in Greece at the Time of Pericles,* London, 1965.

W.G. Forrest, *The Emergence of Greek Democracy. The Character of Greek Politics 800-400 B.C.,* London, 1966.

——, "Legislation in Sparta," in *Phoenix* 21, 1967, pp. 11-19.

A. French, *The Growth of the Athenian Economy,* London, 1964.

A.J. Graham, *Colony and Mother City in Ancient Greece,* Manchester, 1964.

G.T. Griffith, "Isegoria in the Assembly at Athens," in *Ancient Society and Institutions,* New York, 1967, pp. 115-38.

W.K.C. Guthrie, *A History of Greek Philosophy. Vol. 3: The Fifth-Century Enlightenment,* Cambridge, 1969.

N.G.L. Hammond, "The Origins and the Nature of the Athenian Alliance of 478-477 B.C.," in *Journal of Hellenic Studies* 87, 1967, pp. 41-61.

A.R.W. Harrison, *The Law of Athens. The Family and Property,* London and Oxford, 1968.

F.D. Harvey, "Literacy in the Athenian Democracy," in *Revue des Etudes Grecques* 79, 1966, pp. 585-635.

C. Hignett, *Xerxes' Invasion of Greece,* Oxford, 1963.

R.J. Hopper, "The Mines and Miners of Athens," in *Greece and Rome* 8, 1961, pp. 138-51.

A.H.M. Jones, *Sparta,* Oxford, 1967.

D. Kagan, "The Origin and Purposes of Ostracism," in *Hesperia* 30, 1961, pp. 393-401.

J.A.O. Larsen, *Greek Federal States, Their Institutions and History*, Oxford, 1968.

D.M. Lewis, "After the Profanation of the Mysteries," in *Ancient Society and Institutions*, New York, 1967, pp. 177-91.

W. Liebeschütz, "Thucydides and the Sicilian Expedition," in *Historia* 17, 1968, pp. 289-306.

H.B. Mattingly, "The Athenian Coinage Decree," in *Historia* 10, 1961, pp. 148-88.

——, "Periclean Imperialism," in *Ancient Society and Institutions*, New York, 1967, pp. 193-223.

M.F. McGregor, "The Genius of Alkibiades," in *Phoenix* 19, 1965, pp. 27-50.

R. Meiggs, "The Crisis of Athenian Imperialism," in *Harvard Studies in Classical Philology* 67, 1963, pp. 1-36.

——, "A Note on the Population of Attica," in *Classical Review* 14, 1964, pp. 2-3.

——, "The Political Implications of the Parthenon," in *Greece and Rome* 10 Supplement, 1963, pp. 36-45.

P. Oliva, *Sparta and Her Social Problems*, Amsterdam, 1970.

M. Ostwald, *Nomos and the Beginning of the Athenian Democracy*, Oxford, 1969.

R. Seager, "Thrasybulus, Conon and Athenian Imperialism," in *Journal of Hellenic Studies* 87, 1967, pp. 95-115.

R. Sealey, "Ephialtes," in *Classical Philology* 59, 1964, pp. 11-22.

——, *Essays in Greek Politics*, New York, 1967.

——, "The Origin of the Delian League," in *Ancient Society and Institutions*, New York, 1967, pp. 233-55.

E.S. Staveley, "Voting Procedure at the Election of Strategoi," in *Ancient Society and Institutions*, New York, 1967, pp. 275-88.

C.M. Tazelaar, "Paides and Epheboi — Some Notes on the Spartan Stages of Youth," in *Mnemosyne* 20, 1967, pp. 127-53.

R. Thomsen, *Eisphora: A Study on Direct Taxation in Ancient Athens*, Copenhagen, 1964.

W.E. Thompson, "The Chronology of 432/1," in *Hermes* 96, 1968, pp. 216-32.

R.F. Willetts, "Marriage and Kinship at Gortyn," in *Proceedings of the Cambridge Philological Society* 11, 1965, pp. 50-61.

INDEX

124

CONCORDANCE OF INSCRIPTIONS AND TEXTS TRANSLATED